He DID You a FAVOR

He DID You a FAVOR

A Smart Girl's Guide to Breaking Up, Waking Up, and Discovering the **Gift of YOU.**

DEBRA ROGERS

Foreword by Andrea Bonior, Ph.D.

1443 E. Washington Blvd. #169
Pasadena, CA. 91104
hedidyouafavor@gmail.com
info@hedidyouafavor.com

Edited by: Karen Frank and Elizabeth Campbell
Book Cover Design by: Christopher Daniels
Art Direction: Julie Metz Ltd./metzdesign.com
Interior Design by: Maureen Forys, Happenstance Type-O-Rama
Logo Design: JKrew Design/designkrew.com

Library of Congress Cataloguing-in-Publication number: TXu 1-793-559
ISBN-13: 978-0-9910635-0-5

Note: Names, places, and certain details have been changed to protect
identities.

Visit "He Did You a Favor" on the web: *www.hedidyouafavor.com*

Table of Contents

Foreword

A breakup can sometimes send us reeling. Whether we were together for 10 years or 10 weeks, it can leave us doubting ourselves and our ability to ever find enough ice cream (or pork carnitas) to make us feel better. Even if we initiated it, or thought that it wouldn't be a big deal, a breakup can knock us off course in big ways and small.

Nearly everyone has had a breakup that has shaken them to the core. To add to the agony, often times they feel like they should be getting over it better, more quickly, or with fewer tears or obsessive thoughts. They feel that having a hard time with it somehow makes them weak or unhealthy.

As a clinical psychologist specializing in young adults and relationships, I'll be the first to tell you that, if the relationship was meaningful, there's virtually no way to avoid the sting of a breakup completely. And it would probably make you less human if you didn't feel something. But what do you want that something to be? And how do you want to use it to forge ahead?

It's natural for us to turn to our friends for sympathy and advice. A good friend can empathize and help us feel like we're not the loser we think we are in the moment. During my years researching the power of friendship for my book, *The Friendship Fix*, I learned that friendship can be downright magical in its own right. But in the wake of an earth shattering romantic breakup, sometimes even the best of friends can't do much to dig us out of our hole.

For understandable reasons, friends may have a vested interest in seeing us happy—and quickly—and so they sometimes don't really want to delve in deeply with us. When you feel bad, they feel bad; so they want to press the fast-forward button to get us feeling better, at any cost, so often we end up faking it.

Or sometimes, friends are secretly (or not-so-secretly) relieved about our breakup, to the point where they simply can't be empathetic about our sadness. They may be unable to understand why we would still be upset over the relationship. And let's face it, they probably wondered why we were with him in the first place. Or they might be unable to see us without the filter of their own singleness or couplehood, making their reaction to our breakup more about them than us.

Of course, some friends are gems and our very best allies in this situation—hold on to them! But, if time with your gem-of-a-friend doesn't seem to be helping, know that it's not necessarily your (or their) fault. Friends are wonderful and can be our lifeline in the aftermath of a breakup, but just as they were never inside our ill-fated relationship, they can't always understand the nuances of what goes on inside of ourselves as it ends.

Even if your friends are tired of hearing about your "worst breakup ever," or offer very little support, that doesn't mean you're alone. Get to know yourself during this time period and to use it for good, rather than not-so-good (no stalking that girl who posted on his wall). This can lead to one of the most rewarding times of self-growth you'll ever have the chance to experience. Getting to know yourself as an individual, rather than just part of a couple, will give you the chance to understand who you really are, and what you really want.

When we're part of a couple, many times we come to automatically see ourselves relative to the other person. We're short because he's particularly tall. We're cautious because he's particularly adventurous. We're organized because his system for storing clothing involves throwing them on different parts of the bedroom floor. Wouldn't it be great, now that you don't have to be seen constantly in comparison to him, to be able to know who you really want to be, even if it's not particularly organized or cautious?

That's just one of the things you can learn from this time period. If breakups are bound to make you feel something, there's a big and meaningful difference between that something being pure misery, and that something being new understanding of yourself in a way that helps you move forward as a stronger, wiser, and more insightful human being. The latter is a person who knows herself better, and is better situated to take the steps needed to find more fulfilling relationships. Virtually all of us would choose that something.

So how do you get there? The answers to those questions fall much more squarely in your control, and by holding this book you've taken the first step in choosing to make things better for yourself.

But perhaps you're balking at the idea of reading a book to help you. The whole breakup business can tread into downright clichéd territory: from Hollywood endings that have Much-Better Dude Number Two entering stage left the moment Dude Number One is done, to the friends who tell you that somehow now you're simply "better off"— when you haven't showered in three days.

Maybe you think that any kind of "self-help" work comes dangerously close to that aunt of yours who lights incense at dawn each morning. Then there's your gung-ho neighbor's "pillow punch anger therapy" idea that feels like it borders on the ridiculous. But, the very idea of "positive thinking" has you thinking that it positively won't help you—not for this anyway. So if "self-help" isn't helpful, what DO you do?

The truth is that not all self-help requires the lighting of incense or sitting in a position you can't get out of, while you reflect on the "deep inner you." *He Did You a Favor* tells it like it is, for real women going through what you're going through. No sunrise yoga required.

The book is packed with inspiration, motivation, and step-by-step tips to guide you through this important time in your life. Debra Rogers brilliantly shares her own stories, and those of other women, to help you work through all the stages of breakup recovery. In the pages of this book, you will find others who understand exactly what you're going through and you'll come to realize you're not a loser (even if you did eat that entire tub of chocolate chunk ice cream)— and you're not alone.

Debra's insightful and witty book will help you see that it's not a matter of making this period disappear, or ignoring that it even happened. *He Did You a Favor* will guide you to making the most of an otherwise difficult period and help you rediscover YOU...so that you really can be better off. Far more than we can say for ice cream!

Andrea Bonior, Ph.D., is a licensed clinical psychologist, media commentator, and professor. Her book, *The Friendship Fix*, was released in 2011, and she is the longtime author of "Baggage Check," the psychological advice column of the *Washington Post Express*. Her expertise has appeared in the *New York Times*, *CNN*, *NPR*, *Cosmopolitan*, *Glamour*, and *USA Today*. In addition to maintaining a private practice, she serves on the faculty of Georgetown University.

Introduction

A History Of Dating and Breakups

Dumped, ditched, split, separated, parted ways, ended, severed...finito.

It's over.

Maybe it happened last night or maybe you've spent the past few weeks schlepping through the ice cream aisle in the grocery store in your flannel PJs and fuzzy pink slippers hoping the clerks aren't keeping tabs on how many gallons of chocolate chip cookie dough you've bought this month. Hey, at least it's not chardonnay (or is it?).

I totally get it.

You've been camped out on the kitchen floor crying into your empty tub of "chocolate therapy." You feel sad, alone, worthless; trying to decipher how the heck this happened. You've listened to his final message a dozen times, hanging onto his every word like it's your last drink of water on "Misery" Island. You keep thinking that maybe he'll have a change of heart and realize what a colossal mistake he's made and beg you to come back.

I understand exactly how you feel—thick in the forest of "ick"—and I know exactly how to get you out. Because of all my breakup knowledge, there's one thing I know—he actually did you a favor.

Which may sound like one of those trite things that your oh-so-smart girlfriend might say, but it's the truth. You may not believe it now, but you will. That's just what we'll work toward together, as you read this book. I wrote it to help you because I have seen it all.

I've dated guys who needed to find themselves; guys who decided they'd rather be friends with benefits; moochers, including a guy who dumped a Snickers bar on a convenience store counter when I was checking out and said jokingly, "Thanks mom." (ugh); mama's boys; guys who've said, "I'm falling too fast for you and I'm scared" (I believed them); and my super-duper specialty: the quintessential player. Yep. I'm the good girl who was always falling for the bad boys.

I've been on *both* sides of the breakup hammer with producers, promising politicians, professional dancers, prop guys, directors, writers, actors, waiters, store managers, stock boys, musicians, and once, a magician who moonlighted as a donut finisher. Yeah, really.

Through every breakup, I believed every lame-ass excuse, took all their phone calls, cried my ass off, lost weight, and gained weight. After months of sadness and serious self-doubt, I'd pull myself out of the muck and throw myself back into the dating pool, only to get my heart busted again by the same type of guy (more on that later).

Then one day, I finally met my Prince Charming.

With this guy, I believed I'd found true love. He was handsome, charming, and successful. When he proposed, I was sure he was The One. We got married at the Four Seasons in Maui and I wore Vera Wang. Two years later, when I got pregnant, I thought my happily-ever-after was complete...

...until I found out my husband was having an affair. I was eight months pregnant. At that point, he had become my entire world. I had no friends, no job, and no life of my own. All I had was this baby. The one we created together after two arduous years of trying. Now here was this man whom I had made the center of my universe, standing in front of me while my back was literally up against the wall, telling me he wanted out. I couldn't believe it. I couldn't believe the man I loved and cherished would do this to me.

I couldn't believe I had it so wrong.

When my husband left, my self-worth was at an all-time low. My emotions were a twisted mess. I was embarrassed and ashamed about my situation. I'd go about my day, putting up a good front, but the moment I got home, I'd have another meltdown. My life was over (or so I thought).

During much of this time I worked as a voice-over actress in film and television from *Street Fighter* to *Xena: Warrior Princess*. I played tough, kick-ass heroines who battled the most vengeful villains and won, every time. But I was losing the battle in my own life. The bad guy (aka, my ex) seemed to be winning, and I was doing nothing to stop my own self-destruction.

When my daughter was born, everything changed. It changed the way I saw myself, the way I saw my life, and how I was going to live it from here on.

A month later, I woke up one morning and these words popped into my head: "He Did You a Favor." Those five simple words lifted the gorilla of self-loathing off my chest and allowed me to officially move forward with a clear purpose: to let go of him and find myself. I hit the brakes on my self-loathing and began to take charge of my life.

How did I do it? It started with letting go of obsessing about something I couldn't control—my ex and the relationship. Instead, I focused on what I could control—myself. I paid attention to my thoughts, stopped fixating on him, asked for help, and started taking better care of myself. I worked at it every day, rebuilding my fragile self-esteem, until I emerged confident, happy, and loving myself in ways I never had before.

I realized all that cartoon warfare taught me something about standing up for myself. It also taught me not to back down from a challenge no matter how bad it got. I was finally able to seize my sword and become the Warrior Princess I was always meant to be.

It was also during this time that miracles happened. Not only did I have this miraculous, new relationship with myself, I developed one with my ex-husband as well. My relationship with my ex became a new, but different, storybook ending—we became loving, supportive friends who helped each other through our own divorce and now have a terrific co-parenting relationship. Additionally, I got incredible new friends, started writing again, and launched a successful screenwriting coaching business.

My life changed in ways I never imagined. I'm now in a relationship with a guy who treats me like the awesome woman I am (yes, I can say that about myself now without throwing up). I'm doing what I love. And I've got an incredible daughter who inspires me every day.

Which leads me to the purpose of this book; and why it's time for you to read it.

You can do this, too. You don't have to go through years of bashing that heartless husband who cheated, the boyfriend who left you in Italy, or the date-from-hell who made you feel like crap and ducked out on dinner leaving you holding the check. The truth is, obsessing about him only hurts you, keeps you spinning in circles, and prevents you from fully becoming the awesome woman you're meant to be. It's time to break free from being locked in a relationship that no longer serves you.

The truth is you are loved.

The truth is you can overcome anything.

The truth is you are a powerful superwoman.

Even after the most devastating breakup, you can come out a winner, too. And right now is the best time to start because...

He did you a big favor!

This breakup happened in order for you to learn and grow. It happened so you can have a more fulfilling life. It happened so you can learn how to have more satisfying relationships and attract men who'll treat you like the amazing woman you are.

Here's the thing about every guy I've ever dated: I can see now that each of them did me a huge favor. I'm grateful because every experience taught me something about myself and brought me to where I am today—happier, healthier, and stronger than I've ever been in my life. For that I can thank each and every one of them.

Now, if you're still looking for a bitch-fest about the guy who dumped you, then go grab a girlfriend, a bottle of chardonnay, and your breakup ice cream, and have at it— go ahead, get it all out. Then read this book; because this isn't about focusing on what's wrong about your breakup, but on what's right.

So let's get busy healing your broken heart and living a joyful life, instead of killing yourself by drowning in an emotional sea of self-wallowing and shame because of the jerky guy who dumped you, who wasn't worthy of you to begin with. Use this breakup as fuel to empower you, and you will be much better for it. Trust me. I'm living proof. Now grab your sword, Warrior Princess, and let's slash this sucker out of your life.

Part I

Your Super Sucky Breakup

Chapter 1

He Did You a Favor because His Ending Is Your New Beginning.

*Y*ou're devastated by the way he impaled your heart on a dagger. You have his picture tacked to a dartboard in your bedroom where you can throw small arrows at his head every night before you cry yourself into another sleepless night.

You've been dumped, cheated, or screwed over, big time. You're the sucker who fell for a jerk like him. You feel like a total failure. Maybe it's time to just crawl into a hole and die. It's head-spinning thoughts like these that can send you racing to the fridge for that leftover raspberry cheesecake.

But that's what many women do. They cut themselves down to the point where they're just rubbish to be tossed in the trash or recycled into another relationship that eventually gets trashed as well.

On top of that, you probably knew it was coming (that intuitive thing) even if you chose to ignore it. Something else to beat yourself up over. You're in pain, mortally wounded, confused, depressed, and wondering what you did to deserve this. You miss him so much it hurts. You want him back—or you're wishing he'd burn in hell. Your self-esteem has just taken a major nose-dive and you're questioning if you were ever good enough for him. Maybe he left you for someone else, or decided you weren't what he wanted anymore, or he'd just rather be alone right now with his Cheetos and Monday Night Football.

I hear you. I've been there. When my husband left, I thought my life was over and I would never love anyone as much as I loved him. I had breakup depression on top of post-partum depression. I was still injecting myself with Heparin due to my pregnancy, and coming off of the massive doses of IVF drugs, which tripled my misery. I cried. I beat myself up. I felt lost. Vulnerable. The life I had was gone. I went on an endless diatribe, telling myself I was worthless and if only I had done this or that we'd still be together and I wouldn't be alone with a newborn baby, scared out of my mind. I couldn't stop shaking. What was I going to do?

As I look back at that woman on the floor, I wish now that I could write her a letter, telling her that everything will be okay—better than okay. Because she had hit bottom, and the only place to go was up.

You Feel Lost Without Him, but Now You Can Find Yourself

You're going to get through this. It may be hard right now, brokenhearted girl, but do you remember a time when something went wrong and you thought you would never get over it in a million frickin' years? Maybe you lost a job, were screwed over by a friend, or got dumped by another lame-ass dude who also didn't treat you like the super-awesome woman you are. You can and will get over this. How? I'm gonna show you.

But first, we have some serious emotional purging to do, so grab a box of Kleenex...or several.

Start by Throwing Yourself a Stellar Pity Party

These are your Wallow Days, where you get to stay in your jammies, eat gummy bears, and give up showering. Smother yourself in shameless self-pity, and cry your butt off. Make pity pancakes. Do your best pity dance. Collapse into pity mania and don't judge; just get it all out.

Here's why we're crying a river: you don't want to hold any of it in, because if you do, you'll make yourself sick. The first step is to let these emotional toxins move through you and out of your body—then you'll kick them right out the kitchen door and slam it shut. Sayonara. Whew. Relief.

While you're doing this essential purging, hit "play" on your breakup playlist. Get comfortable on the kitchen floor and grab a pint of your favorite frozen indulgence. (Yes, I am suggesting that you devour something super unhealthy just this once, but choose wisely. You could go with Skinny Cow® Caramel Cone or Almond Dream® Cappuccino Swirl. Fewer calories, same result.) Crank up the volume on your breakup jukebox and let the cry-fest begin. It could last minutes or hours—and it may come back around again. You never know what's going to trigger another attack or where it's going to happen. Any little thing can set it off. You could be in the mall and you hear "your song," or you catch a whiff of his Hugo Boss cologne in an elevator, or you pass by the hotel where you went for New Year's Eve last year (that happened to me and I ended up calling a friend, sobbing in Times Square).

> **Breakup tip:** Obsession is a choice—choose not to do it.

But Don't Go down Obsession Road

Grief is good up to a point, but indulge in too much of it and you'll get stuck being a depressionista, drowning yourself in cake batter fudge, watching chick flicks at one in the morning, and tormenting yourself about how you were never good enough. It's this psychological torture we mercilessly inflict on ourselves that causes the most damage. Perhaps you've morphed into this crazy gal who's become:

* **A Master Sleuth**: raiding his drawers for receipts, pictures, notes, bank statements, anything that will confirm what you already know...he's cheating on you.

* **A Champion Clinger**: going through vacation pictures, viewing his FB posts, or listening to his old messages over and over as you desperately cling to the past, hoping there's still a shred of a chance you'll get back together.

* **A Professional Self-Boxer**: beating yourself up mercilessly for all the shoulda-woulda-coulda things you might have said or done that would've kept him

from breaking up with you (It wouldn't have. He still would've done the dirty deed).

I spent many sleepless nights going over how it could've happened and what I could've done differently. It's crazy where our minds go. Was it the fact that I didn't like snowboarding (I was bruised from head to toe after the first day)? Was it that I fell asleep in the car too many times and didn't stay up and talk? Or that I didn't wear my hair the way he wanted me to?

And if we haven't tortured ourselves enough and need to find more reasons to freak out, our thoughts go to the other woman (if there was one), and how much more amazing she must be than us, because she was able to steal him away. You are only hurting yourself with these thoughts. All this negative self-talk does is have a damaging impact on you—it does nothing to your ex at all.

> *Boy, did I hit bottom. I was so depressed that I developed a neurological problem that doctors thought was multiple sclerosis, with lesions on my spinal cord. I know it was directly related to how much of a piece of shit I thought I was, how angry I was at myself for falling for such a crap relationship (again), and how angry I was at him for treating me badly. A year and some odd months later after building my self-esteem back up, my MS-like symptoms finally went into remission.*
>
> *—"Jane"*

What is disease? Dis-ease—an imbalance within yourself. This is what obsessing will get you, so don't do it.

Things We Obsess about When a Relationship Tanks

* We ask: *"Why me?"*

* We put our imperfections under a microscope and dissect them, but we forget what's good about us.

* We are consumed with trying to figure out why Mr. Heartbreaker could've dumped us. Is it something I did? Something I said? Is it because I'm a neat freak, I'm too much of a homebody, or I can't even boil an egg?

* We imagine all the things we could've done or said that would've kept him around. If only I had gone on that rock-climbing trip with him, gave him more space, or learned to speak French.

* We are tormented by thoughts of the other woman (if there is one, and sometimes we make her up even if there isn't) and try to figure out what she has that we don't. Is she prettier than me? Is she smarter than me? Does she have bigger breasts?

* We can't stop thinking about him and what he's doing right now.

Here's another thing obsession does. It warps reality. Soon, you're remembering all the good things about him and none of the bad. He becomes the guy-of-your-dreams and you'll never have another guy as great as him in your whole entire life. And subsequently, you turn into the most worthless, hopeless, loser for not being able to hang on to this ideal gem of a guy.

Finally, don't let your obsession with this breakup spiral you into "all men suck" (they don't), or "I suck" (you don't). Don't let one crappy situation suddenly blow up into *all* the insecurities in your life. Let's deal with this one and move on to all that's good and working in your life instead.

This Breakup Is Your Wakeup Call

It's time to get out of fantasy and into reality. If you were meant to be with this guy, you wouldn't be pulling yourself out of the moat of despair. And while you're still obsessing about how to get him back, he's at an Italian restaurant with a new chick drinking chianti and sharing a string of spaghetti, à la *Lady and the Tramp*. If that visual doesn't want to make you want to cut him loose, how about this: He changed his status to "single" and then unfriended you and all your friends on Facebook. Do you still want to obsess about Mr. Heartbreaker? No? Good.

So here you are sitting in your room, alone and scared. You thought you were destined to be with him forever, but now all you feel destined for is misery and pain. How could this happen? What went wrong? Let's look instead on what went *right*.

> *When I returned from a trip overseas, I was ecstatic to see my boyfriend and share all my stories and adventures. However, upon my return I came across an email from a woman to him. It was obvious by the language within the email that there was something intimate going on between them.*
>
> (continues)

(continued)

Reading it, I felt the words pierce through me. I was shocked, overwhelmed with all kinds of emotions, but most of all I was filled with grief. Just days before, he spoke to me about marriage; how he never felt the need to get married, but ever since I came into his life, he felt differently. He said he wanted to spend the rest of his life with me. Why would someone say such things when it was obvious that he was sleeping with another woman?

I confronted him about the email, and instead of answering me, he made snide comments, and then he did what he always did—run away and hide.

Although I was incredibly hurt, I decided to work on myself for the next few months, and it was one of the best decisions I've ever made.

—"Amira"

You Think You've Lost Your True Love? Think Again.

Here's a reality check: just as this guy was put in your life for a reason, this break up was put there for a reason, as well.

People come in and out of our lives for one purpose only: to help us learn and grow. Relationships give us the greatest capacity to learn. You are meant to find out something about yourself from this experience. Whether you were together for six months or were married for six years, it's about the connection you had with him, how he impacted your life, and how you can both learn and move on to lead more rewarding lives.

> This relationship served you in some way, but it will serve you more by its ending.

So what if the guy who dumped you actually did you a huge favor? That, in fact, he helped you (even if it wasn't intentional) because your relationship with him was complete and it was time to move on to someone better?

> *This guy had a business right next to my hair salon for years, but we'd never met. One day I noticed a For Sale sign in his shop window. He was closing his business. As fate would have it, we bumped into each other that day. Our chemistry was insane. We had two incredible, love-filled weeks together. He even met my parents. I was so certain I'd found The One and that fate put us together.*
>
> *Then, he disappeared. Literally. His shop was cleared out and he stopped calling. I would walk by the empty store on my way to work thinking, "What happened?" For months I kept telling everyone he was "the one who got away." But later, I realized there was no way he could be The One if he just up and left me without a word.*
>
> *—"Trish"*

It's important to let go of limiting beliefs that cause us to judge, label, and try to put our relationships in a neat little box instead of being open to what comes. When someone breaks up with you, you feel hopeless, helpless, or not in control of your life. But you're not hopeless or helpless and you are in control. You can pull yourself out of the ditch of despair and learn something from this. If you don't, you could be doomed to repeat a bad pattern all over again with someone else. Ugh, right? I've done it and I've seen it. Trust me, it's not a fun ride the second time around either.

You can't control what happened but you can control your reaction to it. In any situation, however powerless you feel, you always have a choice. You may think you're stuck, but you're free to choose what to do next. You can be a slave to this breakup and drown in self-pity, or you can be empowered by it. It's your decision. So what're you going to do?

> **He did you a favor because...his ending is a chance for a new beginning for the best person in the world...YOU.**

The Do-Yourself-a-Favor Workbook: Your Sweet, Epic Pity-Party

This "party for one" has an important purpose: to take care of your loving self.

Party Prep

* Get in your favorite jammies (if they have gaping holes in them, who cares—no one's going to see them).

* Put on some serious heartbreaker music.

* Light a few candles.

* Surround yourself with fluffy pillows.

* Wrap yourself in a super comfy blanket.

Food

For dinner: Order your favorite take-out—Chinese, pizza, or whatever comfort food you're in the mood for. Allow yourself some stellar self-indulgence.

For dessert: Treat yourself to dark chocolate. Studies show chocolate triggers sensors in your brain that beat depression and make you feel better (Heck, why not? Unless you're allergic or don't like sweets, it's worth a delicious try.)

Party Games

Obsession Expulsion Game

 * Write down everything you're obsessing about. Don't hold back. Get it all out. Use as many pieces of paper as you need.

 * When you're done, tear them up into little pieces, while saying, "Let go, let go, let go." Toss them in the trash.

Game of Love

 * Write down five things you love about yourself. For example: I love my sense of humor. I love my compassion. I love my creativity. I love how adventurous I am. I love that I'm a great partner in relationships (and I'll find someone better to partner with).

 * Say them five times out loud.

 * Put them on your nightstand and repeat them every morning.

By doing this, you'll begin to shift your focus back to you and what makes you great (and a great catch).

Chapter 2

He Did You a Favor because You Get to Purge Mr. Not Worthy.

It's time to do spring cleaning so you can get a fresh start. Get ready to get your hands dirty (or you may want to slip on some pink rubber gloves) and do what's got to be done. So here goes...

Your Super Helpful Breakup Plan

Here's your path to getting over this guy.

1. No contact. This rule is so important after a breakup. You're experiencing relationship withdrawal and while you may feel that one phone call or just seeing his face on the web will help ease your pain, it won't. It will only send you into pity mania again.

Your ex is not going to give you closure, so staying in contact with him won't help. You won't hear that one thing that'll make it all make sense and make the hurt go away.

And by the way, the no-contact rule applies to his friends and family as well.

To help you stop this madness:

You're now on the do not call list. Don't pick up that phone—to call him or take his calls. If he calls, let your voicemail do the answering for you. You need breathing room here to get perspective. And stop looking for that miracle "I want you back" message. The same goes for texting too. Even a simple "Hi" text is not harmless and definitely not allowed.

> **Breakup tip:** *Important! Don't* delete his number. Instead change his name on your phone to:
> Do Not Answer.

I deleted my boyfriend's number, and a year later he called. I didn't remember the number, so I accidently picked up. It immediately brought up a bunch of old feelings. We had an awkward conversation, which turned into a month of conversations and a dinner date.

Then he stopped calling, and I had to get over him all over again. Now, I've changed his name on my phone to "NEVER pick up!"

—"Pam"

Cut-off email correspondence. If he emails, you delete it. Do not open it. If you do, it'll just open your wound up even more. If he's incredibly persistent and you can't take it, get a new email address altogether and only let your friends have access to it. That's extreme but you have to do whatever's necessary to give you the room you need to take care of you.

> **Breakup tip:** If it's too hard or involved to get a new email address, set his email address to go to your spam folder so you don't have to even see it.

Don't become a master hacker. No breaking into his personal accounts. Or if you already know the passwords to his email, bank account, or his fantasy football account, forget them. Wipe them out of your head and don't log in. Ever. Nothing good can come of it. You may find him flirting with a girl he met online, or his bank account might show a lavish purchase from Victoria's Secret. Logging into anything, even his fantasy football, is a total fumble on your part.

Banish him from your social circles. Pull your face off of his Facebook page, Twitter, Google +, Pinterest, all of it. Block, de-circle, unfollow, and unfriend him. Seriously, do you really need a constant reminder of the guy who tore your heart apart? If you're not ready to unfriend him, then use the "hide" feature so he won't appear in your news feed. But think about it—cutting all digital ties is the healthier choice right now. If you become friends later, you can always add him to your social circles again.

> **Breakup tip:** If you have his password, lose it; don't use it.

Do your own password change. Consider changing your password to something like: "IDeserveMore," "SuperPowerBabe," or "ITotallyRock," so every time you log in you'll be reminded of how great *you* are. Change them up frequently to keep up your personal and emotional security.

2. Purge, purge, purge. Trash it, return it, donate it, or recycle it. Do whatever you need to do to get rid of his stuff. And that means *all* his stuff: photos, books, DVD's, love notes, mementos, whatever's lying around and making you sad. If you can't deal with his stuff yet, pack everything in a box and store it away where you can't see it, or ask a friend to help deal with it. You don't want any reminders of your past relationship hanging around you right now because it'll keep you hanging onto him.

3. Don't starve yourself or gorge yourself. If you do, you'll either pass out or throw up. 'Nuff said.

4. Get a breakup pal. Or get several. Breakup pals are friends or family members who are truly there for you. They call you out on the lies you may have been telling yourself, give you an objective opinion on why Mr. Heartbreaker isn't right for you, as well as give you post breakup support.

These are *not* the friends who'll spy on him for you, gossip online, or who keep telling you, "I can't believe you broke up, you two were so good together." Those kinds of friends will not help you deal while you heal. They'll only add salt into your open wound and prolong the hurt.

When I went back to school to get my master's degree, I felt something was really off with my husband. Soon after, I found out he was having an affair. When I called him on it, he felt very ashamed and remorseful. He told me it had been going on for months.

This was the lowest point of my life. I hit rock bottom. I thought my life was over. I had purpose in my work, but relationships are everything to me. I sunk into a deep, dark depression. I didn't see any hope. I lost all my self-esteem. I felt like a complete victim. And to make it worse, I had just turned 50. I had hot flashes, hot sweats, and my hair was falling out. I felt I had lost everything. I thought, "Who's going to want me now?"

Thankfully, I had a community of people who really, really loved me, including several longtime male friends who just held the space for me. It was a process of realizing that as long as I was breathing, I had a chance to improve my life. It took me a year of constant work on myself. I was determined to see the beauty in this and the healing. This process can be very painful and very adverse, but I learned it's also what makes us beautiful and what makes us so strong.

I'm happily dating again and I thank my friends for supporting me every step of the way.

—"Julie"

Real breakup pals will also keep you in check when you're on your third margarita and about to go home with some biker dude who's covered in tattoos of his ex-girlfriends.

5. It's not about him anymore; it's about you. Our bodies renew themselves regularly, constantly shedding old cells and creating new ones. So when heartbreak occurs why not create a new you as well? Take this as an opportunity to heal, rebuild, and be even better than before. Use this experience to become stronger and more powerful. The fact that you are reading this book shows you have chosen this path of empowerment.

> **Favorable tip:** Your power is in the present; in what you choose to do right now.

From Breaking Up to Breaking Free

Your pity party is over and your power party is waiting for you. It's time to get the heck out of your breakup rut and move toward the better life that awaits you. So get ready for some serious healing. Here are several things you can do right now:

Your "Feel Better Now" List

1. Breathe, baby, breathe. Simply focusing on your breath can do so much. It's great for releasing stress, energizing your body, and getting back in touch with *you*. The best thing is, you can do it anywhere, anytime.

First, sit up straight, shoulders back. Good posture is great for improving your mood. Then, breathe in for five seconds through your nose, and fill yourself up with a nourishing dose of self-compassion. Last, slowly breathe out for five seconds through your mouth. Release any negative thoughts about him or yourself. Do this daily for three to five minutes.

2. Write it down. It's one of the first things I did after my breakup. I have years of journals (it's one of the reasons I wrote this book) and I still journal to this day. Here's what journaling does for you: it allows you to take all the crap that's swirling around inside of your head (giving you a throbbing headache) and get it onto the page so you can get rid of it. It also allows some great inner guidance—we all have it—to come through and help solve problems or release any blocks you may have.

Write a few pages a day, preferably when you first wake up in the morning. It helped me immensely and it still does.

> **Favorable tip:** Take action, however small; at least you're moving.

3. Use self-indulgence to your advantage. Self-care is where we go last. I mean, who has time when we're stuck in pain and pummeling our self-esteem, but it should be first on our daily list. If you don't take care of yourself, how do you expect to get better and find the man of your dreams? (I'm referring to the *actual* man of your dreams, not the sucky guy who just dumped you.)

Taking Loving Care Of You

Here are some ways to pamper your precious self. You deserve some tender loving care right now.

Get a relaxing massage. Stick with a gentle one, please. Don't go for the torturous deep tissue massage. You've gone through enough torment already.

Go for an energizing walk. You'll be exercising and getting some needed fresh air and sunshine after being curled up in bed, sleeping in the same dirty sheets.

Get a nourishing facial. A great facial can brighten your post-grieving face and can shrink those puffy eyes.

Take a refreshing bubble bath. Let Mr. Bubble soothe your aching muscles. If you want, toss in some rose petals and let them refresh your senses.

Take a staycation. Go for a long drive. Grab a coffee and sit on the beach. Have a picnic and sit under a tree reading a great book. See a double feature (maybe dump the chick flick this time and go see an action heroine kicking butt instead of getting her heart stomped on). Hike to a waterfall. Or do a combination of any of these. Just remember, this day's all about you.

Do whatever lifts your spirits. Get creative! Take an oil painting class, or a Zumba class, or go to an outdoor concert in the park and listen to some great music, whatever you're into that makes you happy.

(continues)

(continued)

It's time to get real with you. Immerse yourself in the things you love. You'll begin to get back to who YOU are, what makes you tick, and what you really want in life.

4. Set your mind on the right things. Studies show that meditation can be a huge mood booster. You don't have to be a Zen master at it, or do it for hours. Just 10 to 20 minutes a day is all it takes to tune out the crazy world and tune into your fabulous self. Meditation also taps into that intuitive voice inside of you that says you deserve so much more.

Awesome Thought Changer

Just like you wouldn't keep your nail polish on for more than two weeks, you shouldn't keep bad thoughts around, or they'll chip away at your self-esteem. Not pretty. So let's give your head some relief from the negative banter that's been hammering it.

Make a list. On one side, write down all the negative thoughts you are having. On the other side, write down an opposite, positive thought. Don't agonize over finding the perfect one—just put down the first thing you think of. You can always adjust or add to it as necessary.

(continues)

(continued)

For example:

WHAT YOU'RE THINKING:	WHAT YOU SHOULD BE THINKING:
I wasn't good enough for him.	I'm a great catch and deserve more.
I wasn't worth his time.	My time is oh-so valuable.
He didn't love me.	I love and value myself.

Don't expect your thoughts to change overnight. Just keep practicing and eventually you will turn that Negative Nelly around. Soon, these positive thoughts will define and empower you—and keep you away from the bag of sour cream and onion potato chips.

5. Get your groove on. Make a playlist of power songs that make you feel like you're able to tackle anything. Blast them. Dance. Sing. Go crazy. Just get moving! Or get on the Stairmaster and get killer thighs and a great butt while you're at it. You may even want to grab some weights and pump up those muscles while you're pumping up your self-esteem. Exercise is fab for getting your beautiful heart pumpin', releasing tension, and getting a killer bod for the next guy you date (he's out there).

This is what my friend does to get over a breakup: Every time a man breaks up with her, she buys herself a new pair of shoes and names them after the guy who dumped her. Then she slips them on and walks all over him. It makes her feel better and she gets a little gift for herself out of it too!

—"Shelli"

You will survive this. Acknowledge that you are the most important person in your life. Rally around your awesome self and you'll eventually discover why he did you a favor. You'll probably even come up with several reasons.

He did you a favor because...now you have the opportunity to rediscover your fabulous self.

The Do-Yourself-a-Favor Workbook: Make a Promise to Yourself

Now's the time to make a commitment to yourself.

Go shopping and get a promise ring to signify your love for you (you don't have to spend a lot of money, just find one that fits well and makes you smile when you look at it).

Put it on and promise to be true to you, always. Now say these words out loud:

* "I promise to love myself more, every day."

* "I promise to focus on my strengths, not my weaknesses."

* "I promise to do my best and let go of self-criticism."

* "I promise to set aside some 'me time,' every week."

* "I promise to only date guys who see me for the amazing woman I am."

Chapter 3

He Did You a Favor because His Excuse Is Your Ticket to Freedom.

By now you've initiated your helpful breakup plan, stopped obsessing (if you haven't yet, don't worry, you'll get there), and are beginning the process of getting back to who you are. But there still may be thoughts of him hanging around as you're trying to make sense of it all. That's perfectly normal. If you can further understand this breakup, it'll be easier to move on.

One thing that can hang you up is if he gave you a crappy breakup excuse. Instead of coming clean with his feelings, maybe he used a line like, "I need my space," "I love you but I'm not in love with you," or the king of excuses, "It's not you, it's me."

You may be asking, "Why?" It could be that he was trying to soften the blow. Or he was trying to get away with no come back. Or he was afraid of hurting you. Still these excuses can make you feel 10 times worse. I've fallen prey to these breakup lines and several others in my dating life. In the moment, I believed him. But as the days slogged by and hurt and insecurity set in, I convinced myself that it *was* about me and devoured an entire container of mint chocolate chip ice cream, feeling even worse about myself—and puffy.

> **Breakup tip:** If he gives you a breakup excuse move on, don't hang on.

I've dated men who were masters at cut-and-run techniques. Women want to talk it out, while men want to move on with as little chatter as possible. The trouble is, his excuses are so vague they leave you wondering, "What does he mean, *really?*" They never tell you exactly what the problem is. The real reason he ended the relationship. Consequently, you're left to figure it out on your own. Great... another reason to mentally torture yourself and make up all kinds of new crazy reasons why he dumped you. The truth is, you may never get the full story. So don't go digging for it. It's a waste of time.

To add to the confusion, some men tack on compliments to their breakup excuse, baffling us even further:

* "But I really like you."

* "I have respect for you."

* "You're really nice."

* "I think you're great."

Breakup compliments give us a spark of hope that there's still a chance to get back together, but he's just trying to lessen the sting.

Decoding His Excuses

Many times, you know he's gonna drop one of these excuse bombs before it happens. There's a change in his behavior; he becomes distant, stops holding your hand, checks his phone too many times, whatever. You know. So buckle up girl, cause this is gonna get bumpy; but you can handle it, because it's all about getting past this guy. Let's take a look at some typical breakup excuses and decipher them.

The Top 10 Seriously Lame Breakup Lines

1. "It's not you, it's me." This all-star breakup line is actually the truth. It *is* about him. Still, he's taking the easy way out.

It could be that things are getting too intense and he can't handle it. Even if you're being cool and taking things slow, he may even fabricate a problem because this relationship is preventing him from sleeping with other chicks. If your guy says this to you, it's a cop-out. He's bailing because he doesn't want to be in this relationship.

Do you still think it's about you? Are you going through your laundry list of "if onlys?" "If only I were prettier."

"If only I were more outgoing." "If only I liked Pokémon." You may still think that, if you changed, he wouldn't be breaking up with you. "If onlys" will only get you into trouble. The sooner you realize that, the sooner you can see that no matter what, he would've done it anyway, Pokémon or not.

What he could be saying:

* It's an attempt to shoulder some of the blame, knowing he's the reason you're breaking up.

* He still thinks you're cool and might still want to be friends.

* He wants to keep his options open.

If he's being a fairly good guy and is trying to shoulder some of the blame, don't jump at the opportunity to play the "blame game." Blame keeps you stuck in pain. So if you find yourself caught up in an unending fault-fest, stop. Who's it helping? Who's it hurting? Who's looking bad now? Trust me, his actions are more than enough to condemn him; you don't have to get in the trenches with him. Just hear what he's saying without picking it apart, drowning in unnecessary suffering and popping Motrin to relieve the pain.

When men want out, they want to do it as cleanly and easily as possible. So when he says, "It's not you, it's me," then just take it for what it is. He said it. Done deal. Move on. Also, by acknowledging this you can begin to let go of *any* lame excuse he may have thrown at you.

So let's move on to some other winners...

2. "I love you, but I'm not in love with you." OMG, did he really say that? Ouch. This is like, "I love you, but not in the same way." This can send you into thinking: "Did he *ever* love me?" "Am I not good enough for him?" "Am I good enough for anyone?" Yes, you are. You just fell for the wrong guy. It happens all the time. He may care about you, but he's never going to commit (I told you it was gonna get rough).

What he could be saying:

* He wants to hang onto his single status.

* He's in love with someone else...or he's gay.

* He wants to have sex, but only as "friends with benefits" (punch yourself if you even *think* of going there).

Take positive action and start dating again. Find a man who's truly, deeply, madly *in* love with you.

One day my husband told me, "Maybe we never should've gotten married." I was crushed. He made me feel like our entire marriage was a lie. To make it worse, I found out he was cheating with a friend of ours.

Looking back now, there could've been a million reasons why he said it. But it doesn't matter anymore. Life worked out the way it was supposed to. We've been divorced for years and we're both much happier for it. And I met and married a great guy who's the husband I was meant to have.

—"Terry"

The truth is, you deserve someone who sees you for the magnificent woman you are. He's out there. You just have to let go of this guy first.

3. "I don't have time for a relationship right now." If he cared about you he'd make the time for you no matter how crazy his workload is, how many business trips he has, or how obsessed he is with model rockets. If a man really wants you there's nothing that will stand in his way and keep him from spending time with you.

What he could be saying:

* My job's more important than you.

* I'm not ready to move in with you (and out of my mom's house).

* Time with you interferes with what I really want, which is to stay single.

This busy dude is wasting your time. Don't wait around for Mr. Occupied one second longer. Go find Mr. Available instead.

4. "You deserve someone better." Yep, you do. Still, you may say, "I know what I want, and it's you," or, "Let me decide what's best for me." Really, he's doing you a favor. How should you respond? By saying nothing, thinking nothing, and doing nothing. He's just trying to find the best way to slip out. Do the same. He's telling you that he doesn't love you the way you deserved to be loved. Hear him and *do not* look for a way back in.

What he could be saying:

* ✳ He admits he hasn't been a great boyfriend lately, so he's breaking it off with you.

* ✳ If you keep hanging on, he'll treat you badly. Afterwards he'll tell you, "I told you so."

* ✳ He wants to have sex with other women or he already has.

You *do* deserve someone better—much better. Move on to a guy who's actually deserving of your love.

5. "I need my space." He's suffering from relationship claustrophobia. If he feels caged, all he'll want to do is escape. If he uses this excuse, he's playing his get-out-of-jail-free card. He's either having second thoughts about the relationship or he's thinking of breaking up altogether.

If he wants space, give it to him. No questions asked. By giving both of you space, there is a chance he may realize he really does love you. So having space is good and healthy, but if you're staring at the walls for months and your so-called boyfriend is nowhere in sight, then it's time to date elsewhere. Because if your guy really loves you he won't want to be away from you for too long.

That old saying, "If you love something set it free" is so true. If he comes back, give him a chance. If he doesn't, then thank your lucky stars for getting out of a relationship that wasn't right for you.

> Breakup tip: If he says he wants time, use your time to date.

What he could be saying:

- ✳ He needs time apart to figure out if he wants to keep dating you.

- ✳ He needs to reclaim his man cave.

- ✳ He needs space to have sex with others.

Lastly, it could be that this guy's used to his independence. He may be a pro bachelor who doesn't want *any* chick crowding his space. This type of guy has no interest in changing his single status. I've dated these guys, too, and trust me it's a lose-lose situation. Do your own cut-and-run and get the heck out of there. Give yourself space and find someone else.

6. "I need to find myself." Where has he been the entire time you've been dating? Obviously, he's been in the land of the lost, while you've been present and accounted for. These guys usually have one foot out the door. They're searching for a life that clearly doesn't include you.

I know this hurts, but you can't save him by trying to help him find himself. He has to do that on his own. Maybe he's unhappy in his job, unhappy with his money situation, or unhappy that he's still living like a frat boy with an eight-foot inflatable Budweiser bottle in his living room. You may think if you help him he'll eventually commit. But by doing this, you're giving away too much of yourself. Additionally, if you get involved in his problems, all of his doubts and insecurities will eventually make their way to you. He may even find a way to blame you.

There is a chance he may eventually get it together, but he probably won't come back to you when he does.

What he could be saying:

* He's unclear what he's doing with his life, but he's clear he doesn't want to do it with you.

* He doesn't have a solid reason to break up, so this is the best he can do.

* He needs to find himself having sex with other women.

If he uses this excuse, he's in no place to commit, no matter how hard you try. The solution? Find a man who's knows who he is and what he wants (and that should be you, Miss Fabulous).

7. "You're too good for me." You *are* too good for him. Why? Because he's obviously not seeing you for the super woman you are; or he sees it, but still doesn't want to be in a relationship. This excuse is similar to, "You deserve someone better." And yep, you do. Boot this one out, and let the door smack him and his lame excuse on the way out.

What he could be saying:

* He doesn't have what it takes to be "good" in a relationship, which means being trustworthy, monogamous, and there for you.

* He knows he's gonna hurt you and wants out before he screws up.

* He wants to have sex with unavailable women who are cruel to men.

Keep your "nice girl" status and move on from this bad boy. If he doesn't think he's worth it, then neither should you. If you stay in this relationship you are not doing yourself any favors.

8. "I'm falling too fast for you and I'm scared." He's telling you the relationship is going too fast for him. The question is, is it going too fast for you?

There may be times when you get caught up in a whirlwind romance where you have this crazy connection and you're seeing each other every day. Guys build love through trust. So when you go from a few dates to falling madly in love (which could be just incredible chemistry), then yes, that could scare the heck out of him.

But it probably means that he wasn't expecting to get attached to you. Meaning he was just looking for something casual. This guy's not ready for a serious relationship. I've received the, "I'm falling too fast for you," line and it ended up months later with him revealing his true commitment issues and us breaking up.

Sometimes they add, "I'm not prepared to fall in love." If he's telling you this, don't stick around to see if he suddenly gets a burst of relationship confidence.

What he could be saying:

✳ You're terrific, but I'm not sure you're The One.

✳ I'm not ready for a long-term commitment.

✳ I'm confused about my feelings, but I still want to have sex with you.

Back off from this guy and give you both a bit of breathing room. If he's really falling for you, he'll let you know soon enough. This is serious "valuing me" stuff. As Kelly Clarkson sings, "I want a man who's by my side, not a boy who runs and hides."

Once, in our many intimate conversations, he mentioned that, due to his past, his heart had shut down. However, since meeting me, he said that his heart was starting to open up again and this scared him terribly. I had told him I was scared too, but I was willing take that leap because I knew what we had was something special and real. He kissed me and said, "You're the best thing that has ever come into my life."

Oddly enough, soon after this confession, our relationship changed. He became distant, and sometimes I wouldn't hear from him for weeks. I knew he was working hard on his project, so I let him have his space.

(continues)

(continued)

When he resurfaced from his "man cave," his demeanor had changed. He was sullen, and I was often the recipient of his sarcastic or rude remarks. At times, it felt as though he was in competition with me. I didn't know where this was coming from, and when I would confront him, he'd turn my words against me and say I was being paranoid and hypersensitive.

I felt as though I was with a ghost; he was there physically, but mentally, he was far way. I did everything to try and bring him back to me, but nothing seemed to move him; he was void of any emotion or feelings. He wasn't merely putting up a wall, he was becoming a wall.

—"Tahlia"

9. "Maybe we should see other people." He wants the perks of having you, but none of the obligations. And BTW, if your ex gave you this or *any* excuse in a text, email, or on Facebook, shame on his wimpy self.

His message is crystal clear: he doesn't want to be in a committed relationship. He wants to keep things "casual," which means he gets to have his cake and eat it too. Keep the cake for yourself.

What he could be saying:

 ✳ He not only wants to see other women, he's already scoped a few out and taken numbers.

* He's already dating someone and wants to be guilt-free.

* He may still want to hook up with you, he just wants to have his hooks in other chicks, too.

There is no "maybe" here. Unless you're totally okay with seeing other people (be honest), stop dating this guy. Go find someone who wants an exclusive relationship with you only.

10. "I just want to be friends." You're happily dating this guy and now he drops the "let's just be friends" bomb? Uh-uh. Don't fall prey to the idea that by being friends, he may eventually come back around and fall in love with you. Now's not the time to try to be friends, no matter how much it hurts to stop seeing him. You've got friends. Friends you can go out with on a Saturday night. Friends you can lean on. Friends who make you feel great. Go hang with them, 'cause hanging around this guy will just make you feel bad. Why? Because nothing you do will change the way he feels about you. Instead you'll be constantly reminded that this friendship is not a relationship and never will be.

After some major healing time and letting go of this guy, if you still want to be friends, then read through to Chapter 11 and see if you can.

What he could be saying:

* He doesn't have the guts to come right out and say he's actually dumping you.

* He wants the benefits of your friendship...and to date others.

* He's doesn't want to be your boyfriend, but may be open to casually shagging you.

So many men I know say they've had sex with a girl who was "just a friend." Bottom line: sex does not equal love.

This guy and I had been friends for years and had always been attracted to one another. So when both of our relationships with others had ended, we began dating. There was no doubt we had incredible chemistry and he kept pushing sex every chance he got. I wanted to take it slow because I was falling for him and I didn't want to blow it. We got close many times, but I always stopped it.

Then, he planned a date where we'd meet at this hotel, have dinner, and then take our date "upstairs." He was so sure I'd say yes, he'd already booked the room. But when I said," I just want to take it slow," he said, "Well, maybe we should just cool it for a while and not see each other." My heart sank. I got off the phone and started crying. I thought maybe it was my fault. Maybe I'd teased him for too long and it wasn't fair to him. So, I called him back and agreed to our "sex date."

He dumped me by text soon after saying, "I just want to be friends."

—"Susan"

Bonus Excuse: "I can't get my ex-girlfriend out of my head." Walk away from this train wreck and don't look back. You don't ever want to get involved with someone who's still hung up on his ex. You're not his nurse. You're not here to give him your best bedside manner. You're not here to try and help him get over her. Don't take on the nurturing role here or this guy will bleed you dry. Instead, give yourself a shot of self-confidence and find someone who's emotionally available.

What he could be saying:

✳ He's dating you to try and make her jealous.

✳ He wants to sleep with his ex or he already has.

✳ Seriously, who cares what he's saying. Dump him.

Ridiculously Lame, but True Excuses

Here are two sad, but absolutely true stories of weird-ass men who broke it off with their significant others. Men can come up with crazy reasons, but it all comes down to the same thing: he doesn't have the confidence to be completely honest with you, and he'll do any moronic thing to get out.

I dated this guy and we hit it off right from the start. After a while, I started thinking he could be The One. But three months into the relationship he suddenly broke it off. He told

(continues)

(continued)

me that an astrologer said he would meet the woman of his dreams in September. Since he met me in May, I couldn't be The One. He said he had to break it off with me so he could be available for this "astrological girl." I never found out if he met his "star mate" or not.

—"Keisha"

And check this one out...

I dated a magician who used one of his magic tricks to break us up.

We had planned for me to bring my family to his home in the mountains for a long weekend so they could meet and spend some quality time together because our relationship was "serious." Within a half hour of our arrival, he insisted that we all play a card game, which I thought was odd. After the game, he magically made a piece of paper appear, as he might present a deck of cards or reveal a dove in his hand (he was always so dramatic). The paper listed the people who'd played the game before. Next to each name was a score. The very first person on the list was his old girlfriend. Without saying anything, I pointed to her name and looked at him, only to receive the tirade of why he had been unfaithful and why he slept with her.

Within an hour, I was driving my family down the mountain away from this "master" magician. It was the last time I saw him, and I never spoke to him again.

—"Mandy"

When He Makes You Break Up with Him (aka, "Super Sucky Dude")

Some guys aren't man enough to even use a breakup excuse. Instead, they'll do things that make you question their commitment. Actions speak louder than words. His actions are giving you the same breakup excuse. He just doesn't have the guts to say the words. If you're picking up on his "I'm not as interested in you anymore" signals, trust they're true. If you choose to ignore his behavior, it'll only get worse. He may even get angry that you're not "getting it." And he'll keep acting badly until you are forced to break up with him. This may leave you with regrets. You may feel you screwed up somehow. I'll tell you right now, if he's acting shitty towards you, he's definitely not The One.

What he could be doing to get you to do the dirty breakup work:

* He stops being affectionate in public.

* He gets shifty about making plans with you.

* He's forgotten your favorite latte, even though he's ordered it a million times.

Also what he's not saying can be just as telling:

* He stops complimenting you.

* He avoids any topics involving you moving in together.

* He stops saying, "I love you."

Pay attention to the signs he's giving you. They're there if you look. Don't sweep them under the rug, hoping they'll go away. He's behaving badly for a reason. Sweep him out of your life and begin with a clean slate.

Finally, never let his words or actions burn you. Instead let them fuel you to find a much better guy. A guy who'll build you up with compliments, not cut you down with excuses.

> **He did you a favor because...his lousy excuse sets you free to find an honest-to-goodness man.**

The Do-Yourself-a-Favor Workbook: the "He Sucks, You Don't" Workout

Put on some classic girl-power anthems such as Aretha Franklin's "Respect," or Gloria Gaynor's "I Will Survive"—because you will.

Grab a firm pillow and punch the heck out of that sucker. Get out all of your frustrations. Use your best kick-his-butt moves. If it'll help, tape a picture of your ex to it for added benefit.

Once you've exhausted yourself...

Hug the pillow (not him, the pillow!) and say, "Thank you." Be grateful you are out of this relationship that's been beating you down.

Now, go take a nice, long bubble bath. Light a candle and visualize letting go of Mr. Wrong and the better future you will have because of it.

Chapter 4

He Did You a Favor because Mistakes Can Be Rockin' Opportunities.

After a breakup, here's another way we obsess: punishing ourselves for the terrible wrongs we think we've done. "Why did I say that? Why did I do that? What was I thinking?" We feel we've made a terrible mistake and by gosh we're going to castigate ourselves for it. Who is this helping? Definitely not you, girlfriend. Who is this hurting? You, you, and...oh yeah, you.

I Screwed Up, Big Time

Nothing kills self-worth faster than self-criticism, and we all can be masters at it. It's funny how many times we'll make excuses for our guy, like "He's really going through a tough time," "He's just so busy," or "He's not a good communicator," but we won't do it for ourselves. Instead, we'll take our self-criticisms to the max, so we're not only idiots for texting him so much, we feel worthless as well. Now, where's that ice cream?

Hating and blaming yourself for the wrongs you've done in your past relationship will also throw you into panic mode. It'll cause you to do regrettable things like leaving "take me back" notes on his apartment door, or sending emails detailing all the reasons he should give you another chance, or posting old pictures of the two of you on Facebook with captions like, "We're meant to be together." Desperate actions such as these are driven by fear and denial. They can damage your already crumbling self-esteem in the worst way, when what you really need is to build it up.

Here's another thing about criticizing your slip-ups—you're torturing yourself about how to change the past. Fixating on what could've been, if only you'd done things differently, will only cause you to drown in guilt and regret. It'll make you stuff yourself with Hershey bars until your stomach aches. You can't go back no matter how much you want to. Regret not only keeps you wedged in the past, it takes away from your life right now, where there is a great opportunity for new experiences.

> The relationship wasn't working—if it was, you'd still be together.

Here's where you're making the biggest error: in thinking you did something specific to end this relationship. You didn't. If you were meant to be with him, he would still be asking you out. If you were meant to be with him, you would've worked out any problems in the relationship. You didn't make that one super colossal blunder that got rid of him—it's just not possible. So please give yourself a break.

> If someone wants to break up they'll find a reason, whether it's a good one or not.

How you acted in the past was a reflection of who you were at the time, mentally, physically, and emotionally. How you act in the present reflects who you are right now. So it's not about what you did when he left; it's about what you're going to do now to learn something about yourself.

> **Favorable tip:** What you need right now is self-love, not self-criticism.

I Know He's Making the Biggest Mistake of His Life, Why Doesn't He?

Do you think you know him better than he does? Are you sure that by breaking up with you he's going to fall into regret and despair—if not now, then sometime, somewhere, when he least expects it? Do you know unequivocally that you're meant to be together, so you have to show him what a huge mistake he's making?

I moved in with this guy, even though I knew he was going through a really rough time. He had no job and was unhappy a lot. But I loved him, so I fell into the role of care-taker. I paid the bills, got him into therapy, and was there for him every step of the way.

After three years, he landed a high-paying corporate job and was feeling good about himself again. Soon after, he tried to break up with me. I was so angry. I said things like, "I saved you." "I'm good for you." I was so convinced we were meant to be together; I kept hanging on. Finally, he told me point blank to move out. He even helped me pack. It was awful.

Looking back, I can see no matter what I said or did, it wouldn't have mattered. He was done. He wanted out. I wasted a lot of time trying to get him back instead of just moving on.

—"Theresa"

You don't need to help him understand how much he has broken your heart and ruined your life. It won't do either of you any good and it won't change anything.

Arguing with your ex about leaving you and making him feel guilty for his actions is like a kid throwing a tantrum over having a toy taken away. Did your parents ever reward you by giving it right back? Probably not. You won't get your boy toy back either.

I thought I was in a happy marriage, until I found out my husband was sleeping with a friend of ours. We had two kids, so we went to see a therapist to try to save our marriage. The therapist asked my husband, "How much does each one of you want to work this out? What percentage? Ninety? Fifty? Ten?" He could never answer that one question. Yet that didn't stop me from doing everything I could to save my relationship. I continued to catch him in lie after lie. I confronted him, threatened him, and gave him ultimatums. I thought if I just kept at it, he would eventually see the error of his ways and come back to me. I even confronted the other woman and told her flat out to stop seeing my husband.

For a year I flip-flopped back and forth between trying to repair what was broken and punishing him for how much he was hurting me. I hacked into his email and checked credit card bills. When he moved into an apartment, I drove over and spied on him, so I could catch him in the affair I already knew he was having. All I can say is that love makes us do stupid things.

One day, I woke up and thought, "What am I doing?" I stopped my behavior, divorced my husband, and moved on. Years later, I met and married a wonderful man. We have a son together and I'm happier than I've ever been.

—"Laurie"

The Mistakes He Says He Sees in You

Not only did he just rip your heart out, he also tells you he thinks you're too clingy, too ambitious, or too much of a flirt.

Sometimes when a guy breaks up with you he decides this is the perfect opportunity (meaning he can walk away and not deal with the aftermath) to tell you mistakes he thinks you made, or all the reasons he broke up with you. Really? Do you want a knife with that? Let's twist it deeper into your already bleeding heart. I've had this happen and it seriously sucks. After receiving an emotional phone call from my ex, which started with, "Why did you give up writing?" and spiraled into other mistakes he thought I made in the relationship, *all* my insecurities surfaced. I thought, "How in the world could I have screwed up so badly?" That one phone call literally brought me to my knees. I cried on the kitchen floor for weeks. I wanted to change the past so badly. I wanted another chance to do it right.

So, as if I wasn't depressed enough, I pummeled myself about writing, too. What made my misery worse was that I'd not only lost him, but also precious time. This caused me to delve even further into self-loathing, because I was older and I thought I was never going to have my dream career. But one day, a friend said something that turned it all around. She said that even if I had become successful in my profession during our marriage, he would've found another reason to have the affair. Who knows what it would've been, but it would've been something. That was a huge revelation for me and allowed me to release any guilt I felt. Only then was I able to pursue my dream career, because, trust me, it's never too late. Ever.

I'm telling you right now, you don't have to take his verbal criticism. Don't be his personal punching bag. Instead, hang up on him. Delete his long-winded emails. Get rid of his texts. Then, go kickboxing and throw some punches yourself. Or get a massage to soothe your battered ego. Or have a date night with friends who make you feel like a winner. Heck, why not do all of them?

> *Favorable tip:* Don't get hung up on the past, instead let the past change you for the better.

This Is Your Golden Opportunity, Not a Missed One

Let's remove the "miss" from mistake. Remember, you didn't miss out on anything. If you didn't make mistakes, you'd never learn anything. So use this as an opportunity—what are you going to take away from this experience?

What you do now is so important because it will define the next phase of your life. Here's what I did, and also what I'm asking you to do: take an honest look at all the "mistakes" you think you made. This isn't for you to go down Beat-up Road crying, "What's wrong with me?" Don't put yourself through the spanking tunnel game. No judgment whatsoever. It's important to look at these mistakes with loving detachment. Here's why you want to look at them— it allows you to recognize any negative patterns in your behavior, to learn from them, and to find ways to improve. This process helps you to become an even better you, filled with positive thoughts and actions.

So let's get working on you and all the things you think you did wrong, so you can get some awesome, positive perspective here. You'll gain so much more by seeing these blunders as "good to know" instead of "kill me now."

> Mistakes are not roadblocks, they're just bumps in the road on your way to a better life.

Let's call these mistakes you think you made *opportunity mistakes*, because remember, this situation is giving you a golden opportunity to learn, heal something within yourself, and become empowered.

Before we can do this, we need to first tackle those niggling, ridiculous mistakes you think you've made.

Stupid Mistakes We Think We Made

Those shoulda-woulda-coulda thoughts can make us perpetually nuts. So let's take all the trivial mistakes that may be driving you insane with unnecessary worry and get them out. Let it rip. This is about purging all your little freak-outs so you can finally get rid of them.

Write them down, and when you look at them, say to yourself, "This is crazy-talk." Toss them and go for a jog, go to the spa, or go shopping. Treat yourself to whatever feels good (and no, it's not that quart of Chubby Hubby). Here's some crazy-talk examples you can permanently unload:

* I should've lost 10 pounds.

* I should've worn my hair in pigtails more.

* I should've gotten a tattoo.

* I should've learned to play *Call of Duty.*

* I should've nagged him less about working too much.

* I should've had sex with him 10 times a week.

* I should've said "like" less.

* I should've learned how to cook, not microwave.

* I should've been kinder to his pit bull.

* I should've let him display his Batman figures in our bedroom.

Now make your list.

Take an honest look at it—do you really think any of those were the definitive reason for your relationship ending? What if a friend gave you this list? What would you tell her? Let them go? Oh, yeah. Tell yourself the same.

Now that you've let go of the crazy talk and the petty screw-ups you think you've made, let's get into opportunity mistakes. Remember, these mistakes did not break you up, so don't go back through the spanking tunnel. This is to show where this relationship did you a favor by teaching you something about yourself.

Opportunity Mistakes You Can Learn From

Let's look at some mistakes that are about your own personal growth and not how well you can cook. Again, we are looking at these mistakes for you, not him. And don't write them down. That's giving them too much power. Remember, they're just giving you the opportunity for further growth.

> There are no mistakes in relationships, only lessons.

So Little Red Riding Hood, where did you lose your way? This is about loving what is, and taking personal responsibility. Don't be a victim of circumstance. Instead, take the reins. Turn these opportunity mistakes into truth and understanding and get on with your awesome life.

Opportunity Mistakes: the List

Opportunity Mistake # 1: Being too critical of him and/or yourself.

Opportunity Mistake #2: Lacking self-confidence.

Opportunity Mistake #3: Constantly comparing yourself to him or others.

Opportunity Mistake #4: Dumping your friends for him.

Opportunity Mistake #5: Being too jealous.

Opportunity Mistake #6: Not setting healthy boundaries.

Opportunity Mistake #7: Not communicating or asking for what you want.

Opportunity Mistake #8: Not being honest with yourself.

Opportunity Mistake #9: Thinking a relationship will solve all your problems.

Opportunity Mistake #10: Hanging onto this relationship when you knew it was over.

Again, don't fall into self-criticism. No one's perfect. If you didn't make and learn from your mistakes, you wouldn't be the person you are today.

Where His Jerky Behavior May Have Messed You Up

Okay, here's the one place where you get to dump some accountability on him, because your mistake could very well have been a reaction to his shitty behavior. But don't take this as an opportunity to show up at his apartment and go psycho-ex-girlfriend on him and key his car. It's just good to know. Remember, we choose our partners to learn something about ourselves based on where we are in our lives.

How Did This Relationship Cause Me to Fall into Unhealthy Patterns?

I once dated this guy who told me he didn't want to be mothered, and complained that his last girlfriend took control of his life. So in the beginning of our relationship, he happily did everything. But after a while things began to change. He got too busy at work to handle even the most mundane things like paying a bill. He wanted to take a trip, but grumbled that he didn't have the time to plan it. He wanted to redo his kitchen, but complained he didn't have time to find a construction person. So I asked if I could help out. He said, "Yes," so I took over several things to ease his daily burdens. After a year, I was handling everything for him. Guess what happened? Yep, it backfired. It's not surprising that "mothering" came up as one of the reasons for our breakup. Looking back, I see how I screwed up, but he encouraged it. No blame on either side, though. What I learned is that there's a difference between being a supportive partner versus a mother hen.

In relationships, you may think your intentions are good, but they might not be well received by your partner. The truth is, people give and receive love differently. You may go in with the best intentions, but still fail. It's no one's fault.

Additionally, couples sometimes adopt habits of their partners, both good and bad. You're vegan, but he's on the Carnivore Diet. After six months with him you find yourself ordering double-double burgers with extra cheese. Or you're friendly and outgoing, but he's a serious couch potato. Eventually, you stop going out altogether and spend endless nights eating take-out and watching *Seinfeld* reruns. Or he's incredibly impatient and soon you're the person who's seething at the grocery store wanting to throw your frozen bananas at the lady in front of you who's taking way too long to check out. After your breakup, you may realize that what you've been doing or how you've been acting is not who you are. Whatever unhealthy habits you may have adopted, now's the perfect time to change them. He did you a favor.

Repeating Our Mistakes, Relationship after Relationship

The definition of insanity is doing the same thing over and over again and expecting different results (Einstein was a smart cookie).

Take a look at your past relationships—do you see any recurring unhealthy patterns? Have you had the same issues come up over and over? Some examples are:

* Do you always choose guys who are emotionally unavailable?

* Do you always choose guys who are controlling?

* Do you always get attached to a guy too soon, only to have the relationship crash and burn in the worst way?

* Do you always focus on your boyfriend's successes more than your own?

* Are you always seeking his approval and not validating yourself?

In my relationships, my helper attitude got me too caught up in my guy's needs. When my boyfriend Tim was having financial problems, I covered most of his bills and practically went broke. When Kurt was having trouble with his screenplay, I gave him free script coaching and stopped writing myself. When John wanted to expand his business I helped him every step of the way and had no time left for me. My missteps were tied into self-worth—I felt that my partner's needs were more important than my own. Additionally, by taking over my boyfriends' lives I emasculated them in some way, which was never my intention. The big lesson I learned: being a helper is who I am, but I don't need to give and give at the expense of myself.

Repeating relationship mistakes keeps you stuck in bad situations, cuts down your self-esteem, and causes you to choose unhappy paths.

My boyfriend was really charming, but he was also unavailable, and could really be jerk sometimes. When he started getting bigger in the music scene, girls would fall for him. He stayed loyal to me, but would throw it in my face a lot—he got off on chicks chasing him all the time. At that point, I began to get really insecure. I'd push him and test him, and he'd push me and test me. Eventually, that's what the relationship became. It was me pushing my boundaries to make sure he wouldn't go, because I was so frightened he was going to leave. And he was on the other end, pushing my boundaries to see how far he could go before I finally got up and walked.

My actions were cries for attention, or ploys to make him jealous. Or sometimes I'd just get sad and wanted him to be there. If I got sad enough, it would work.

Then the fighting started. I would always come at him with the "how could you's?" I played the victim role really well. If we were in public, he'd be arrogant and rude and belittle me. And he would shut down all the time, because he knew if he did, I would lose it. We were like oil and water.

Finally, I left him. It was these bad behavior patterns I had to break free of (as well as break up with him) in order to be truly happy.

—"Ally"

No One's Needs Are More Important than Yours

It's always important to take care of your needs first. It's like the safety instruction they give you on airplanes: put your mask on *first* before assisting others. You are no good to anyone if you can't breathe.

How a Mistake Can Turn into an Empowering Self-Revelation

Remember, mistakes give you an opportunity to grow into a better you. This is also your golden chance to treat yourself better and find someone new who'll treat you better too. Here's how to change a negative pattern:

* Identify what you're doing.

* Recognize why you're doing it.

* Let go of ANY judgment.

* Make a positive change.

* Ask for help if you need it.

So, if you always get attached to a guy too soon, give the next guy some breathing room and devote yourself to your own interests instead. If you always focus on your boyfriend's successes more than your own, start working toward your goals. Stop being his one-woman-cheerleader. Instead, cheer yourself on. If you're always seeking his approval, find ways to validate yourself. Gather a group of friends and family who love and support you and share your accomplishments with them.

It's important not to criticize yourself while you're trying to change a negative pattern—you may even make mistakes while you're getting there. You've probably spent a lifetime cultivating this behavior; you can't expect it to just go away in one night. If you're having trouble, ask your friends and family for support. Or ask for help from a counselor or therapist. Most of all, be patient with yourself. The biggest thing is recognizing it's there and that it doesn't go with the fabulous gal you're becoming.

Accept everything about yourself, even your mistakes. They're part of who you are. So make no apologies. Have no regrets. In truth, there really are no mistakes. There are no super, colossal blunders. Only lessons. You are always in the perfect place in your life.

> **He did you a favor because...by learning from your past, you'll leap into a better future.**

The Do-Yourself-a-Favor Workbook: Clean out Your Mental Closet; or, How to Stop Piling Up the Junk in Your Head...and Clean It out Instead

It's time clean your mental house and have a yard sale!

1. Get rid of all those old, worn-out thoughts cluttering up your head. Just like you wouldn't wear the same shoes you had when you were 10 because they don't fit you anymore, lose the negative self-talk that doesn't fit you either. It could be tough to toss because you may have been carrying it around since you were a kid, but it's just old chatter and it doesn't go with the fabulous woman you're growing into.

2. Look at your cleared-out mental closet and see what beautiful thoughts are left. These are the ones that make you feel great and show off your best assets like, I'm smart, I'm outgoing, I'm funny, and so on.

3. Now that you've freed up some space, take a little me-time shopping spree and add some new, happy thoughts to your closet. Make sure these are thoughts you would comfortably wear. Think about how courageous, creative, or caring you are. Have fun thought shopping!

And just like a great blouse is even better when paired with a great pair of jeans, combine these thoughts to make them even more awesome. Mix and match and see what you come up with. For example:

* I'm caring and smart.

* I'm sensitive and courageous.

* I'm playful and confident.

4. Maintain your mental closet with these happy thoughts.
What's important is that they fit your own personal style.
Wear them every day.

Now that all the thoughts in your mental closet make you
feel fabulous, you'll go out into the world radiating confidence—and attracting better relationships.

Part II

Your Relationship Resume

Chapter 5

He Did You a Favor if You Were Dating Mr. Toxic.

Surviving a breakup is worse than having food poisoning. But what if he'd been poisoning you all along, and the real you has been dying a slow and painful death in the relationship?

Let's put it another way. Would you eat the apple from the witch if you knew it was poisoned? Would you stick your hand in a rattlesnake's mouth and let it bite you with its lethal fangs? Then why would you ever be with someone who fills you with insecurity, distrust, or anger?

In order to move forward in a powerful way, look back at your ex and see what can be learned, and if he was Mr. Toxic, how you can stop poisoning yourself.

Seriously, wouldn't it be good to know so you're not doomed to destroy your self-worth again with next guy you date?

The Irresistible Toxic Man

Have you ever had a chocolate donut you knew was bad for you, and then a week later you forgot and did it again? We may know Mr. Toxic is wrong for us but we date him anyway, because we can't stop the addiction.

And why do we date these toxic men to begin with? Because on the surface they can be sexy, charming, and tons of fun. And once we're hooked, it's tough to let go. We'll keep focusing on the good and turn a blind eye to the bad, no matter how bad it gets. Yes, we date them and sometimes we even marry them. We drank the toxin, and now, with Britney Spears's "Toxic" running through our heads, we drown in our own poisoned paradise.

> Being attracted to a toxic guy is like being a moth attracted to a bug zapper light, eventually you're gonna get burned.

So who are these lethal men we fall into the Venus fly trap with? It's important to know how to spot them so you can avoid getting screwed. Here are some we tend to fall for, who pretend they're Clark Kent when really they're Lex Luther:

Nathan, the nasty nitpicker: he'll constantly criticize your hairstyle, your mole, or how you can never load the dishwasher right.

Pete, the perennial player: the look-don't-touch rule doesn't apply to him. This high-stakes lady-killer will pounce on the next pretty woman who smiles at him.

Sam, the sly saboteur: he'll do anything to wreck your perfect date night.

Clayton, the cantankerous controller: he texts, "Where r u" 20 times a day.

Larry, the perpetual liar: he told you he was working late, and *yes* that means three in the morning, and that perfume you smell is really his new aftershave.

Nick, the neglectful narcissist: occasionally, he'll stop talking about himself so *you* can talk about him, too.

Toxic men pull us into their deadly fantasy and we go willingly. We believe they're the man of our Cinderella dreams. But soon those warning signs creep in. We hope that nagging inner voice telling us to run will go away, but it keeps getting louder. Instinct is your best friend. It's your beacon. It'll always guide you while you're navigating rough waters, so, for your sake, swim toward it.

Your Warning Signs

You can spot warning signs even on the first date if you know what to look for. So let's look at the guy who just dumped you and see if those yellow lights were flashing from the beginning.

Yellow Light

Be cautious if...

 ✳ He nitpicks about the dress you're wearing.

* He trashes his ex-girlfriend.

* He communicates with you exclusively by text.

* He says he's always had trouble with commitment.

* He talks too much about a co-worker, but insists they're "just friends."

What Do You Do if that Yellow Light's Flashing?

Tell him. It's important to express how you feel. Don't suppress your emotions. Always remember, you are most important. If you're able to work it out with him, great. If not, chalk it up to experience. There are seven billion people on the planet and half are men. You'll find someone else.

If he nitpicks, voice your opinion the moment it happens, not weeks later. This has always been a tough one for me, but I've gotten much better at it. When you nip it in the bud right away, he'll see it, get it, and hopefully not do it again. If he does (and it escalates), it's time to say, "Bye-bye, bottom-dweller." We criticize ourselves enough; do we really need any help?

He trashes his ex-girlfriend. Okay, she could've been a psycho, but be careful with the complainers. Because chances are you'll be on the other end of that in due time. It also says a lot about him and how he views women. I dated this guy who slammed his ex-girlfriend at dinner one night. He said she was a "bitch" who was a "control freak" and "insanely jealous." Later I found out this was coming from a narcissistic non-committer.

If he only communicates by text, change it. How? Simple. He texts, you call. Keep the pattern going, until he realizes you'd like some verbal contact, too. Make your point, but don't make a huge deal out of it. He'll get the message because you're not ramming it down his throat. It could be he's a social media freak and has to relearn how to personally interact. If he's the right guy, he'll make the effort.

If past commitment issues come up, talk about where he is right now. It could be he's in a better place and is ready for commitment. Keep checking in from time to time in an informal, non-fussy way. If the same warning sign keeps coming up, then cut him loose. Find a guy who'll be exclusive.

If he talks a lot about a girl at work, see that yellow light and proceed with caution. Ask questions. Observe his behavior. Listen to your instincts. They'll be able to tell you if he wants to act on it or if they really are just friends.

Red Light

You're in the danger zone if...

* He's cagey about making plans with you.

* He's a stage-five clinger who keeps bugging you to dump your friends.

* He's constantly checking messages from the same chick and ignoring you.

* He criticizes you openly in public.

* He's less attentive to you after you've had sex with him.

What Do You Do if that Red Light's Flashing?

Stop. Don't pass go. If you were the one for him (and he for you), he wouldn't be behaving badly, treating you badly, or making you feel bad about yourself. Don't believe the good and ignore the bad. If you do, it's going get ugly. What makes it difficult is that nasty cuddle hormone oxytocin that, like it or not, causes us to bond with Mr. Toxic after sex. Your hormones are coursing through your love veins and before you know it, you're completely hooked. You obsess about him, desperate to get your next "fix." Give yourself a dose of self-confidence and get the heck out.

Who's Your Addiction?

Mine's been the perennial player. I dove into that toxic pool without looking, heart wide open, and smacked my head on the bottom more than once. Did I learn from it? Yes and no. As I got older, I became aware of my dating habits, but I also became a good game player and thus kept Casanovas circling around me for years. Fun and games is fun, but ultimately my heart lost. What's more astonishing is I was surprised every time one of those relationships ended.

Dating toxic men is like playing the lottery. You fantasize about how great it's gonna be when you win, but when you lose, you play again, hoping next time will be different. This can go on forever—with you never winning. Don't leave your dating life up to chance. Choose to play somewhere else with someone who gives you much better odds.

> *I was living with my college sweetheart. The first year, it was sunshine and roses. We'd stay up all night staring into each other's eyes. We couldn't get enough of one another.*
>
> *Then he started belittling me in small ways. During arguments he'd find a way to call me a name about something he knew I was sensitive about: "fat," "ugly," "big nose"— he even called me "mole face" at one point. At least once a week I would leave our apartment sobbing.*
>
> *One day during a 70s theme party we were hosting, a friend came in. Her outfit was so spectacular, I called across the room for him to see it. He was in the middle of conversation with someone. I called once more. And over the whole crowd, he yelled out, "Shut up, bitch!"*
>
> *Silly 23-year-old girl that I was, I hadn't learned that love didn't require me to put up with that. But despite the fact that I was still incredibly in love with him, I forced myself to move out.*
>
> *I'm now in a relationship with a guy who makes me feel good about myself and I'm so much happier.*
>
> —"Jennifer"

How Toxic Is this Relationship?

Toxic relationships can go from mildly offensive to all-out emotionally, and sometimes physically, abusive—from the mild narcissist to the monster abuser. (If you're in the latter category, you are deep in the danger zone, girl. Get out and get help.) Gather your support team (friends, family, therapists) to help you get through this. They'll also give the emotional support you need to break free from Mr. Destructive.

You've Been Poisoned If...

Your self-esteem is at an all-time low.

You dump your friends and only hang out with his.

Your needs are always taking a backseat, while his are always in front.

You catch him in lie after lie but do nothing about it.

You're feeling insanely jealous.

You're getting sucked into his drama and it's making you feel sick.

Toxic Self

What we think of ourselves is what may have gotten us here in the first place. We're missing something in ourselves and so we crave it from a guy who can give us that false high. Getting into a relationship with someone because you're looking to fill a need in yourself is never good. Additionally, if you go into a relationship already feeling bad about yourself, you'll attract a man who brings that out in you. Some deadly self-esteem killers are:

I'm not pretty enough. My nose is too big. My hair is too curly. My eyes are too close together.

I'm not smart enough. I suck at Trivial Pursuit. I can't figure out Quicken. I've read all the *For Dummies* books.

I'm not sexy enough. My boobs are too small. I have a muffin top. I have legs like SpongeBob.

I'm not good enough. I'm not talented enough. I constantly compare myself to others. I never get what I want.

I moved to San Francisco where my old friend Matt was living. We delved into a romance that consisted of him saying, "Jump," and me asking, "How high?" I thought he was my *Harry* from When Harry Met Sally. However, *unlike Harry,* Matt got stoned four to five times a day, and constantly lied or avoided the truth with me, while he continued to sleep with his ex-wife and countless other women that year.

When I finally asked him point blank if he ever saw us having a future together, he said, "I've never been happier with a woman in my life than I am with you. The sex is great, I love that we're emotionally intimate, and you're one of my best friends; but no, I'm not in love with you and I don't see us having a future together." So, I was brave and ended both the friendship and the sex-ship.

—"Liz"

What Do We Do Wrong When We're in a Toxic Relationship?

1. We don't listen to our intuition. It's that sixth sense that signals something is terribly wrong. Maybe you had a horrible nightmare and woke up in a cold sweat, or suddenly had a sinking feeling in your gut. Intuition can see through all the smoke and mirrors. Be still and listen to that inner voice. The smoke will clear and you'll be able to see the real truth.

2. We hear only what we want to hear. When he says that he and a coworker are "just friends," yet he can't stop talking about her, you believe him, no questions asked.

When he says he's "confused" about the relationship you think, "If I try harder he'll come around."

When he throws veiled insults at you about your job, your new haircut, or your cat, you think he's just in a bad mood or he really doesn't mean it.

When he says the reason he never invites you over is because his place is not as nice as yours, you think, "When we live together it won't be a problem."

3. We decide we can change him. You can't—and he doesn't want you to.

4. We make excuses for him. He's too busy for me because he's working for a promotion. Or, he criticizes me because he wants me to be a better person. Or, he doesn't want to get married until he makes six figures... or wins the lottery.

Breakup tip: Don't blame him; leave him.

> *It came to a point where our relationship was so toxic, I would have chest pains. My self-esteem was hindered in a huge way, but I kept it a secret. Finally, I decided to be honest with myself or else I would become one of so many women that would just sweep problems under the rug.*
>
> *After I left him, I realized how big and strong I really am; without having left him, I would never have known.*
>
> —"Anna"

You may hold out hope that he's just going through a phase, and if you hang in there, he'll come around. Hang on to your self-worth instead.

How to Detox

You're in the treatment center now. You know you have an addiction to this guy, you know your role in it, and you are asking for help. Good for you! It's time to stop being the victim and start being the victor.

> **Favorable tip:** The antidote is to have love and compassion for yourself.

What to Do

1. Step out of denial.

2. Pay attention to your own emotional needs (and know that you don't need anyone else to complete you).

3. Practice letting go of any toxic feelings associated with this guy.

4. Remind yourself of how great you really are.

5. Get out of isolation. Lean on your friends; they can be your biggest champions.

Always remember, relationships reflect back to us aspects of ourselves. So take a look in the mirror and see what your toxic man is reflecting back to you. Is it an unhealthy self-image? Is it a lack of belief in your talents? Is it a desperate desire to be needed? Now, fair queen, begin to change it by changing your thoughts about yourself. By building a healthier relationship with yourself, you'll attract better relationships with others.

And by the way, get rid of those toxic friends as well. You know them; those jealous, sabotaging, gossipy vixens. And say goodbye to frenemies, whose quicksand behavior will drag you down in a heartbeat. They're not doing you any good either. They're only adding fuel to an already out-of-control fire, which is burning up your self-esteem and leaving ashes for everyone to stomp on.

Remember How Amazing You Are

The most important thing here is to keep remembering how awesome *you* are. Post phrases around your place to remind you and read them every day. For example:

✳ I believe in my talents.

✳ I value my worth.

✳ I am confident and creative in everything I do.

* I am capable of achieving my goals.

* I'm a great catch and am deserving of a better guy.

Keep feeding yourself daily doses of self-love and you'll crave more loving relationships (and friendships).

He did you a favor because...you are finally out of a toxic relationship and are ready to move on to a healthier you!

The Do-Yourself-a-Favor Workbook: Your 28-Day Detox

Experts say it takes about 28 days to detox from sugar, so let's take the next 28 days to detox from your love addiction. It may take longer, but if you hang in there, you'll get there.

Over the next four weeks, do the following:

1. Identify the toxic men you keep dating.

    Remember them—the cantankerous controller, the sly saboteur, neglectful narcissist and so on? Those guys who make you feel incredibly insecure or bring out the worst in you?

2. Recognize (and accept) why you do chose them.

    Are you with Mr. Cantankerous Controller because you are more afraid of being alone than being in a bad relationship? Are you with Mr. Neglectful Narcissist because you feel you're not good enough or don't measure up in some way? Are you with Mr. Moocher because you thrive on being needed?

    Don't judge yourself. We are not here to prove, we are here to improve, so cut yourself some slack.

3. Replace the bad habit with a good one.

    If you are afraid of being alone then be around those who love you. Have friends over for game night, have weekly dinners with your family...or adopt a dog.

    If your self-worth is suffering, then do something that inspires you. Paint in the park, take a pottery class or go to an art exhibit. Spending quality time with yourself is so valuable. And if Mr. Toxic asks you out again, you can tell him, "I have a date." And you do—a better one with yourself.

Also, who knows, you may bump into Mr. Fabulous on your "me date."

If you're a relentless giver, try receiving for a change. Let a friend, coworker, or even your sister do something nice for you, like run an errand, pick up the lunch tab, or help you clean out all the junk that reminds you of your toxic ex (if you haven't done that already).

4. Stay away from your addiction.

The best way to stop addiction is to not have contact with it. So definitely stay away from your ex. And if you see any of those toxic signs in a guy you're attracted to, stay away from him, too.

Also, don't jump into another relationship just for a temporary feel-good fix. If you do, and the red flags start waving, pinch yourself really hard to remind yourself to walk away. You have the willpower to stop this addiction.

5. Get yourself a support system.

Gather a few close friends who'll kick your butt if you get involved with another toxic guy. They'll tell you when you're slipping back into denial, making excuses, or losing yourself in another bad relationship. Listen to them and let them help you break free from this destructive habit once and for all.

The stronger you get, the better you'll be at holding out for an awesome, loving relationship.

Chapter 6

He Did You a Favor if You Were Dating the Wrong Type.

*Y*our relationship with Mr. Right has gone terribly wrong, but was he really right for you to begin with? Your ex may not have been toxic; he just may not have been the right type for you. Again, by understanding this breakup, you'll be able to make better choices in the future.

So let's get into the reality of Mr. Heartbreak Boy. Instead of seeing this breakup as a loss, see it as a near miss, Miss Fabulous! You didn't get further involved with the wrong guy. This is not only about getting over your ex, it's about looking at your dating style so you can land someone who's really right for you. And remember, chemistry can put blinders on you in a heartbeat and have you ignoring those warning signs. Leave chemistry at the door for now. This isn't about thinking with your hormones, but with your heart.

Was He Really Your Type?

Have you always been attracted to the lone wolf, and yet wonder why you can't ever get him to settle down? Or you dreamed of the Ken to your Barbie, but you feel incredibly insecure when you're with him? Or you say you want someone who's intelligent and treats you well, but keep dating the opposite, because of the sexual connection? Grab some ice and cool down the burning chemistry, and you'll see what you're missing, and why what you've been doing hasn't been working for you.

> I dated this guy who was gorgeous and seemed very sweet. The morning after we slept together, he pulled out a stack of scrapbooks filled with his modeling pictures. Then, I found out his mother was upstairs and he was still living with her! I couldn't get my panties on fast enough. Bottom line—looks aren't everything.
>
> —"Lynda"

What's on the outside is not necessarily what's inside. The wrapping may look good, but the interior could be something completely different. He may seem like a funny, cool guy everyone loves, but you later find out that he won't let your friends come over, or he never turns the funny off, or you can't have a real conversation with him. Or you may be attracted to his wit and intelligence, but then you find out that he speaks passive-aggressive fluently, doesn't introduce you to his friends, and spends more time playing video games than playing with you.

Hotties You May Want to Cool Off on (and One of Them May Be Your Ex)

Many of us date a guy's potential, and not the guy who's in front of us. We think if we hang in there, he'll eventually give us what we need. But it's like looking in a shop that has everything you want, but is closed for business.

The guy who's all personality and no substance. He's great at parties, but not so good with one-on-one.

The guy who's all about nailing you in the sack. He's sexy, lives in the moment, and pushes your boundaries because he can.

The working guy who'd rather date his computer. He's more interested in working himself to death than living a great life with you.

The guy who seems like a great catch, but doesn't want to be caught. He's hot, fun, and totally unattainable.

The guy who'd rather spend time with his mama. He calls her every night before he goes to bed, values her opinion over yours, and tells you that your lasagna is *almost* as good as hers.

Observe his actions, not what he's telling you. If he's not willing to give you what you need then find a "man shop" that's open, and well-stocked with what you desire.

> **Favorable tip:** Listen to your intuition, no matter how good he looks in those jeans.

Which Type Was Your Ex?

Did you know deep down that he wasn't right, but thought you could change him? Or, think that this time would be different? Did he seem adorkable, but was really just a dorky mess? By looking back at what didn't work for you, you'll be better prepared next time. This breakup is giving you the opportunity to clear your head and discover that maybe your dating habits aren't the best, or that some changes can be made.

How do you know? Here's one simple way. Ask yourself: Do you keep dating the same type of guy who always breaks your heart? If you answer "yes," then it's time to rethink your dating habits.

> **Helpful tip:** if your type is making you unhappy then your type is unhealthy for you because you're basing it on your weaknesses, not your strengths.

What's Your Type Based On?

Similar to dating a toxic man, if you're dating the type of guy who's self-righteous; or nitpicky; or who wants sex, but has no respect for you, then you're not valuing and appreciating yourself. Shove his sexy butt out of bed. Own your star power, and choose a guy who makes you feel awesome, and not like you're a take-out burger at McDonald's. Don't get hung up on the superficial—like the fact that he's a great kisser—and ignore the deeper issues. Your body falls in love faster than your brain; by then it may be hard to determine if this guy's really right for you.

Distinguishing who your right type is comes from being super honest with yourself. It's like trying on a fabulous pair of shoes that you think are perfect, except that they're too narrow for your feet. You love the way they look though, so you walk around the store thinking, "It's not *that* bad, maybe they'll stretch out." So you buy them. The first time you wear them, they still pinch, but you think you can handle it because you love them so much. But after a while, your feet get sore and you get painful blisters. Now you're really hurting. Are you still going to keep wearing them or find a pair that fits you better? The same goes for your man. If you ignore the pain he causes you, it'll only get worse. Instead, find a man who fits you better.

So in order to find the man you want, you have to figure out who *you* are and see if it's a good match. If your personalities don't match, don't adapt to make the two of you fit. It's like a puzzle. You take two pieces that look like they should fit, but don't, and you try to put them together anyway. You bang that puzzle piece with your fist. You squish it, jam it, but no matter how hard you try, it just keeps popping back out. It's not going to work.

Don't Pretend to Be Something You're Not

Don't pretend be a devil-may-care woman to snag a man when you're really a homebody who likes to cook and stay up late watching old movies. You have to be authentic to who you truly are. Why? Because it's gonna come out in the relationship at some point. He may think you're a jet-setter who's cool with keeping things casual, when really you want a relationship with someone who wants to settle down and have kids. If you put on a persona to please him, eventually it will crack and your real self will show through. By then, you may have fallen in love with him and you'll be destined to get hurt.

> *Andy was into wine, so I became wine connoisseur. I studied up on wine-making, and spent a ton of money buying a shit-load of wine that's still crammed in my closet.*
>
> *With Danny, I got into comics and action figures, and would spend hours with him in comic book stores, learning what he liked. I became an online expert at finding and buying rare Japanese anime figures.*
>
> *With John, I became an expert in environmental issues, and would educate myself on the importance of Danish plant farms.*
>
> *Imagine all I could've accomplished if I put even half that energy into myself; what I wanted and what I was passionate about?*
>
> —"Mary"

What Are Your Deal-Breakers?

This is a good time to reevaluate what it is you desire. Knowing who you are and what you want out of a relationship by looking back at the guy who dumped you and how he made you feel is the first step. It all comes down to self-love. How much do you love yourself? How much do you value yourself?

> *After my divorce, I knew it was going to be an opportunity for me to get very clear on who I was, what my values were, and what I wanted, because my eyes were so wide open. I started to feel optimistic that I had a chance to blossom into my own life and to experience my own financial freedom. Also to find a relationship with a man who I could be full with emotionally, financially, and successfully.*
>
> *My breakup freed me to move into the life I came here to live—which was a full life in every way.*
>
> —"Nancy"

Here's your chance to get crystal clear. To honor the amazing woman you are. Take a look at this past breakup and see where you may have compromised at the expense of yourself. Or where you may have fooled yourself into thinking you two were a match when you actually weren't. Or where you put up with ignored phone calls, his workaholic schedule, or his constant judging. This is the time to look at things that you may have done or accepted with your ex that didn't feel good to you and to set healthy boundaries for the next relationship.

> **Favorable tip:** A relationship should bring out the best in you, not the worst.

Your List of Negotiable Wants vs. Absolute Deal-Breakers.

There's the short list of deal-breakers, but there's also the long list of wants. It's important to remember as you're making your deal-breaker list, that you may come up with a bunch of wants that are negotiable. I don't want you to be a hard-ass or a stick-in-the-mud. This is about clearly defining your life, but not being petty about every single thing. No one's perfect. We all have little annoying habits.

I have a girlfriend who's doing online dating, and is very clear about everything she wants in a man, right down to his hair color. She's sticking meticulously to it, and thus is not leaving any room whatsoever for a fabulous guy to come into her life, because she's too focused on controlling every little detail.

Once, I tried to set up another girlfriend of mine with this terrific guy. Her first words were, "Let me send you my list, and see if he meets my criteria." I told her to stop being a control freak and just have coffee with the guy. It's good to have standards, but let's not go crazy here. Leave room for good, old-fashioned spontaneity and maybe, just maybe, you'll be pleasantly surprised.

Negotiable Wants

Here are 10 things you could give on:

1. He should be taller than me.

2. He should've graduated from an Ivy League school.

3. He should have six-pack abs and no chest hair.

4. He should always use correct grammar.

5. He should be exceptionally neat and clean.

6. He should drink coffee. The real stuff, not those girly drinks.

7. He should be a Type A...or B, but hard working.

8. He should read Science Fiction novels.

9. His wardrobe should consist of Armani and Hugo Boss.

10. His income should be in the high six figures. (It would be nice but is it a real deal-breaker? And financially stable doesn't always mean emotionally stable. I'm just saying.)

If you're still hung up on any of the above, then it's time to loosen up, Miss Picky, otherwise you may be buying yourself a one-way ticket to Lonesome Town. Don't immediately nix him if he's into exotic foods, still owns a flip phone, or doesn't have a Facebook account.

How Do You Define What Your Deal-Breakers Are?

Ask yourself three questions:

1. What do I require in a relationship right now?

2. What am I willing to put up with?

3. What will I absolutely not put up with?

> Who is your type? The guy who gives you what you require.

When making your deal-breaker list, don't get caught up in what you don't want. It's like if you want to lose weight, you don't focus on that box of jelly donuts, right?

Possible "No-Breaking" Deal-Breakers

Here are 10 deal-breakers from my interviews with women. See if any of these are yours. If not, write yours down and stick to them:

1. He must get along with my friends.

2. He must be supportive of my career goals.

3. He must be a one-woman man.

4. He must want kids.

5. He must respect me.

6. He must love my family.

7. He must like my dogs (they're family too).

8. He must want to get married.

9. He must be kind.

10. He must be willing to compromise.

Some of these may sound like no-brainers, but you'd be surprised how many times we look the other way or are too quick to forgive when our guy violates them. The problem is, when we're fully engaged in a relationship with someone, we'll sometimes conveniently "forget" what our deal-breakers are and try to pretend (meaning lie to ourselves) that they're not such a big deal after all. But trust me, they'll bite you in the end. And when you break up, your memory will miraculously come back and you'll remember what they were and then kick yourself for not sticking to them in the first place.

Your deal-breaker list shouldn't be long, but it does have to be absolute. Be truthful with what you require from a man, so even if Mr. Super Sexy shows up on your doorstep, armed with your trusty list, you'll know that if he's not right, he's not right. If you ignore your list, you'll be ignoring those red flags as well, as you drown in his dreamy eyes. You'll be saying to yourself, "Who cares if he doesn't want to have kids." Or, "Who cares if he doesn't like me to hang out with my friends." Or, "Who cares if he doesn't compromise." Don't develop an "I can live with it" attitude, because if it's an honest-to-goodness deal-breaker, you can't.

Favorable tip: Don't let a man determine what you want. Decide for yourself and stick with it.

And remember, never make excuses for him like, "He's just super jealous because he loves me," or, "He's just really stressed at work, that's why he's so distant," or, "When he gets his MBA, PhD, and wins the Nobel Prize, then he'll settle down." You could be waiting a lifetime for him to change and missing out on the fabulous guy you could be having beautiful babies with!

> *I'm getting so much more honest and I love it. I don't waste time any more when it comes to dating. I know what I want. I require a man who reflects who I am. If it's not there, then it's not a match.*
>
> —"Marlene"

Is He Really the Marrying Type?

When it comes to "tying the knot" we often think our boyfriend can't commit because we did something wrong or there's something wrong with us. But it could be that he's just not ready. Or he's just getting out of a crappy relationship and you're Miss Rebound. Or he may be one of those rare guys who never wants to get hitched. It sucks, I know. But listen to your gut. See the signs. He's giving them to you for a reason.

A friend told me this story: after a year of dating, she gave her guy an ultimatum—either he would commit to her and move the relationship up to the next level or she would leave him. He said no, so they broke up. For years afterward, she agonized over the fact that she had possibly made the biggest mistake of her life. She felt that if she'd only just let the relationship play out, they'd be married by now. She believed he was "the one that got away." But when the guy was asked about their relationship, he just shrugged and said they dated for a while and broke up. He said it was "no big deal." No emotion. No lingering thoughts of her. Nothing. She was not for him and never would be. In that case, she did herself a huge favor.

If your ex was not into getting married, then thank your lucky stars you're out of that relationship. He did you a favor. Now, wish on a star for your marrying man!

> *There's compromise and there's compromise. That's what I did for years and so did my ex. Now I feel like I'm in spiritual boot camp and I'm learning where I should never compromise. I mean, I can be tolerant of many things and can be adaptable, but I can't do that with my deal-breakers anymore.*
>
> —"Regina"

Compromise is good, but never ever put your needs on hold for a man. You'll regret it and will eventually resent him for it or blame yourself.

So if your goal is to get married, don't fall into a relationship with Mr. Utterly Uncommitted, because no matter how hard you try, getting married won't be on his radar. Instead pick Mr. Monogamous, Mr. Family Guy, or Mr. Ready-To-Put-A-Ring-On-Your-Finger.

Rewriting Your Dating Type

Now that you know who you are and what you want, it could be time to break your dating pattern. Maybe it's time to give Mr. Nice-Guy-Who's-Not-Your-Type a shot. He may be a better fit than you think.

If you date against your normal type, you may feel uncomfortable at first. You may question it, especially if you're used to dating guys who dump their problems on you, don't listen to you, or blame you for everything. If that's what you've been comfortable with then change it! Set a higher standard. Check out the guy who could be standing right next to you. You know the type. He's the one who treats you well, who cares about you, and wants to make you happy.

If you take the plunge and date against your normal type, don't go looking for problems either. My girlfriend did that and it cost her a great relationship. She was so used to the bad boys that when she finally dated a sweet guy, she went looking for trouble and eventually caused them to break up. Afterwards she said, "See? He wasn't right for me." She sabotaged a good relationship and dived back into another series of bad relationships and breakups.

> *For years, I dated men who played mind games and were phenomenally uncommitted. Until this nice, cute guy asked me out. My girlfriend said, "Wow, he's hot!" My first words were, "He's not my type." I was actually considering setting him up with her, but then he asked me out. I said, "yes," thinking he could be a good friend. He ended up being warm, kind, and surprisingly sexy. We've been dating two years now and our relationship is beyond anything I ever dreamed of. I'm so in love and he makes me happier than anyone I've ever been with.*
>
> *—"Tammy"*

Am I saying that Mr. Self-Righteous will never change? Or Mr. Serious can never loosen up? Or that Mr. Free Spirit is never going to want to get married? No. If you really want to give him a shot, go ahead. Just proceed with caution. Be prepared to leave if he's violating your deal-breakers, if there's no hope of fixing it, or he doesn't want to fix it.

So who's the next person you're going to date? Are you going to repeat old patterns or take a chance with someone new? Will he be another emotional vampire or be gentle and loving? Will he be a guy who criticizes you, or one who really gets you? Will he be another Casanova, or a guy who's totally committed to you. Get super clear and get busy discovering a great-fitting guy for you.

> **He did you a favor because...now you get to find the right guy for you.**

The Do-Yourself-a-Favor Workbook: Date Right for Your Type Nutrition Book

1. First, define your right type.

   He's a guy who:

   * Shares similar values.

   * Shares similar beliefs.

   * Shares similar interests.

2. Use your list of deal-breakers.

   Memorize them. Keep them in your purse if you have to, so if a guy isn't respecting your privacy, or won't hang out with your friends, or lies to you, and it's a deal-breaker, then you better hit the pause button on this guy and cross him off your dating list.

3. Based on your deal-breakers, make healthier choices.

   Choose a fresh selection of men who nourish the best in you, make you feel great about yourself, and give you a boost of energy. For example, he's a guy who:

   * Is passionate and loves trying new things.

   * Is helpful and considerate.

   * Would rather talk to you than Twitter.

   He's a guy who's not only right for you, but is great with your friends, too.

4. Keep this healthy pattern going.

   If Mr. Wonderful starts to show his true colors three months into the relationship and those red flags show up, don't backslide. Remind yourself how bad you felt after being with the last Mr. Judgmental, Mr. Moody, or Mr. Wandering Eye. Consult your friends, if needed, to help keep you on a healthy track.

5. Don't overanalyze this new man diet.

   Go with it for a while and see how your dating life changes and how much better you feel about you.

Chapter 7

He Did You a Favor if He's Being Mr. Flip-Flop.

*Y*our boyfriend broke up with you a month ago but then texts you to say he's thinking of you, or calls to say, "I really miss you," or he shows up on your front lawn with a boom box, playing a cheesy song. You take him back (you're a sucker for cheesy songs) and he dumps you again. Three weeks later you get another text, saying, "I can't stop thinking about you." OMG. This type of breakup-makeup-breakup cycle can really mess with your head and keep you stuck in pain. I know. I did it for a year with a guy I was in love with. Eventually, he left for good and I was left with a bigger heartache.

The truth is, your ex's "I want you back" actions don't necessarily mean he's coming back. Frequently, it's a knee-jerk reaction to being upset about the breakup (yes, even though he dumped you, he may be feeling bad). His actions could mean several things, such as:

 ✳ He doesn't want you to be mad at him.

 ✳ He wants sex.

* He feels bad about what he did.

* He *really* wants sex.

* He really wants his Third Eye Blind CD back.

In most cases, he really doesn't want to get back with you; he just wants a temporary fix. Whether he's conscious of it or not, he's playing with your head. As hard as this is to deal with, it's important to recognize that your guy's post-breakup behavior is preventing you from breaking free.

What Mr. Flip-Flop Could Be Doing

1. He's sending you emails, texts, or personal messages on Facebook. It's his way of communicating with you without connection or commitment. Maybe he still wants to be friends (you're not ready). Maybe he drives by the sports bar where you used to hang out and feels the urge to call you. Or he's feeling a bit lonely and just wants to talk. Seems harmless, right? Wrong. His actions can easily send you spiraling into that dark tunnel again, just when you are beginning to see the light.

There are three reasons for his texts (and I've experienced them all):

1. He wants to go out (warning: this "date night" usually leads to breakup sex).

2. He wants a midnight booty call.

3. He doesn't want to actually see you he just wants to hear from someone who cares about him.

This resurfacing guy is operating exclusively on his terms, because...

✳ He needs a quick ego boost.

✳ He still cares about you, but is keeping his options open to make sure he doesn't miss out on someone better.

✳ He cycles through women—he spun the roulette wheel and your turn came up again.

✳ You're his back-up girl when things go bad with someone else.

✳ You had great sex when you were dating, so why not just keep doing it?

2. He doesn't know what he wants, but he thinks it's you. He wants you back and then he doesn't. He loves you and then he's not sure of his feelings. He wants to meet for dinner, and then cancels three times in a row, only to call you again (and BTW, why are you taking his calls?). You want to believe him so badly. He may be saying things you want to hear, things that are giving you hope...but it's false hope.

He may also contact you because he just has to get something off his chest, or he's trying to work through his emotions. He should talk to someone else, not you. You're not the one he should be working out his emotions with, and vice versa. You're not his breakup friend; you're his brokenhearted ex-girlfriend. Right now, you're trying to get over him and his actions are not helping at all. This is just another way for Mr. Flip-Flop to mess with your head.

> **Breakup tip:** Second thoughts will give you a second heartache.

3. He left something at your place. I don't care if he left his favorite Hurley t-shirt (which you better not be sleeping in), his Calvin Kleins, or his Breitling watch, there's no reason for him to contact you 10 times. He needs it back? Great. If you haven't already tossed it during your "pity party," then mail it to him and eat the postage fee. Your emotional healing is worth much more than a few bucks. Or set up a time when you're not there and leave it in a box on your doorstep. Or have a friend, your neighbor, or your sister leave it with one of his friends (because you don't want to see them right now either) and have him pick it up there. You should do whatever it takes not to see the face of the man who broke your heart.

I had this shirt from a guy who broke up with me, and it sat in my closet for weeks. We made plans several times for me to return it, but our plans always fell through. I even had the shirt dry cleaned (what was I thinking?)! All this back-and-forth was keeping me from moving on. Finally, I had enough. I mailed it back. Done. Over.

4. He's showing up at your place. He's confused. He just needs to "see you one more time." He really needs those Calvin Kleins back. No excuse is a good one. Whatever the reason, if he's showing up unannounced, he's not playing fair, because every time he does it sets you back.

Five Fab Uses for the T-Shirt He Left at Your Place

1. Make a doggie blanket or a cat toy.

2. Restyle it into a workout shirt. Cut the neck (like *Flashdance*) and wear it while you work out and get a killer body. Think of cutting him out of your life.

   Note: wash it first and get rid of his smell. You don't need your senses to remind you of him when you're trying to forget. And don't wear the shirt if you're thinking it's him wrapping his arms around you. If that's the case, toss it.

3. Reuse it as a cloth to polish your car before a fabulous night out with your girlfriends.

4. Use it to clean the floors you camped out on during your pity party. Clean him up and out of your life and get clean floors, too. That's multitasking!

5. Make a tote bag. Then take it with you grocery shopping for the dinner you're going to make for that new, hot guy you're dating.

Your ex won't give you what you need, but he doesn't want to lose you either, because he's still getting something from you (love, adoration, sex, an ego boost). These are temporary until he finds someone else who can replace those things. Then you'll be left in the dust again, wondering what the heck just happened—only this time you'll feel 10 times worse.

5. He's trying to get you into his bed...or any bed. Don't ever mistake sex for love and commitment. Men are single-focused. Sex is sex. Now that he can't have you, (because remember, he broke up with you) you are suddenly more alluring to him. You are the forbidden apple. The hot girl he was first attracted to. He wants to make sure you're still into him, without having to commit. Again, if you give in, he'll keep calling until he finds someone else. And then the calls will stop.

I had a long-distance breakup, which turned into a year of plane flights and sex in hotel rooms. We did it in New York, Boston, Connecticut—we did it all up and down the East Coast. But nothing ever changed. After a while, I got tired. I didn't need to take a six-hour plane ride to get some lovin'. It was temporary love anyway—it never meant what I hoped it would.

You're Only Hurting Yourself If...

1. You take his calls, or you respond to his texts, messages, or emails. Remember, his occasional messages are just a noncommittal way of communicating with you. They're those fleeting moments when he's thinking about you and may want to get together for a quickie, but those moments disappear just as quickly. Dispel the fantasy that you can hang out with him right now. Instead, throw a cold washcloth on your face and chill on this guy.

2. You attempt to destroy his love life. Okay, you had a moment of weakness and checked his Instagram. You saw a pic of him locking lips with an unknown blond chick. Your heart thumps. Your throat gets that lump in it. How could he do that so soon after your breakup? Despite everything, you're still harboring thoughts of the two of you getting back together and now this chick is in the way. He should be with you, not her. You have to do something. You have to get rid of her. You have to get him back. Whoa. Put the brakes on this impending train wreck. Don't get involved in his love life, *ever*. Even if you accomplish a minor victory the major defeat will be yours, because nothing you do will ultimately stop him from dating other women.

3. You attempt to destroy his life in general. The same goes for making his life hell just to punish him. Don't post embarrassing pictures of him on Facebook. Don't spread nasty rumors about him. Don't gossip about him to coworkers. Ultimately, you're punishing yourself. Even if he made you go through a mean, public breakup, don't sink to his level. Sabotaging him only damages you. It keeps you focused on what's not working and away from what is, which is your new rockin' life.

> Breakup tip: The best revenge is living well, not destroying his life.

4. You use, and excuse, any reason to contact him. You are not doing yourself any favors if you contact him for any reason whatsoever, no matter how innocent or harmless the reason seems to be. If you do, you're still thinking *way* too much about him and it's a way of staying involved with him.

I dated this guy who was a big foodie. After we broke up, I'd still text him about a cool recipe I found or a hot restaurant I discovered. What harm could it do, right? A lot. I was still thinking way too much about him (and eating too much, as well). It was a way of staying connected to him, which was the last thing I needed to do.

> **Breakup tip:** His interests are not your concern anymore. *Your* interests are.

Additionally, if you contact him, one of three things will happen:

* He'll respond nicely but politely (giving you false hope).

* He won't respond at all (making you feel horrible).

* He'll tell you to stop contacting him (making you feel even worse).

But what if you need to contact him because he has something that's yours? The same rule applies. Unless it's your purse, laptop, or cat, let it go. Leave it and all the emotions attached to it behind. It's a bummer, I know. I left my favorite hoop earrings at this guy's place. We traded emails every few weeks and kept making and canceling dinner plans. This went on for months. Finally, I had enough. I let go. I couldn't take all this pointless back and forth. It wasn't doing either one of us any good. The lesson? Unless it was your great-grandmother's diamond earrings, leave the jewelry at his place and go buy yourself a more fabulous pair.

If you absolutely have to have those earrings back, have him leave them with a friend of yours or mail them back to you. Let *him* eat the postage this time.

5. You have breakup sex. One hot hookup on a Friday night (or Tuesday because he's saving his weekends for new dates) can set the clock back on your healing. Do you really want to risk having to start all over again? I get it. It's tough. Your heart's vulnerable. You believe sex will somehow make things better. You believe having him "just one more time" will help you get through this breakup easier. Sure it feels great in the moment, but what about later? It's like eating a plate of double fudge brownies—if you considered the disgusting, bloated feeling you'd have the next morning, you might think twice before taking that first bite. The same goes for breakup sex. Don't set aside all the great healing you've done just to briefly relive the good times. You'll end up with that icky "I have to take a shower" feeling when he's gone the next morning and nothing's changed. It sucks, so don't do it.

6. You take him back. Are you absolutely sure? Are you clear on what you want and don't want from a relationship? If you answered, "Yes," and you're willing to give him another chance:

> **Ask yourself: Why are you taking him back?** First of all, I'm not going to judge if his "I want you back" actions are sincere or not. I can't see his face. But I

am taking a stand with you. So I'm asking you to sit quietly with yourself and get super clear.

Be honest, are you taking him back because...

* You don't want to be alone?

* You're still hurting?

* You're sad, a lot.

* You miss his dog?

* You think getting back together with him will fix what's broken in your life?

If so, these are temporary fixes, not long-term ones. Let me put it this way: if your car keeps breaking down, do you want a mechanic to patch it up so you can just get on the road again? If you do, chances are it will break down again. And each time you'll get more frustrated and upset. How about trading it in for a new model? Think about it. If it's not working, why keep driving it?

If you really want to take him back... Some guys say they didn't know what they had until it was too late, and they mean it. If you absolutely believe this is your guy and he's willing to commit and work on improving the relationship, then give him a shot. Just be cautious and smart.

If you want to give him another chance, put him on "relationship probation." "Relationship probation" means you're going out with your friends, doing things you love, and focusing on your goals. It means having lots of "me time" and less "him time." During this probation period be on the lookout for any reoccurring red flags (you should have them memorized by now)—if you spot them, you are not authorized to go forward.

The truth is, if he's man enough and serious enough, he'll do every darn thing to get you and keep you. If he's not up to the task, he may repeat his pattern and dump you all over again. Just be prepared for anything, so you don't fall back into that black pit of despair.

What if I take him back and it happens again? Don't beat yourself up if it doesn't work on the second go-around. Sometimes we need additional confirmation that he's not Mr. Right to finally cut him loose. Don't berate yourself for giving him another chance. It could be that the lessons between the two of you weren't done yet. Now they are, so give him the final heave-ho. Move on surer than ever that he's not the one for you. He did you a big favor. Now you definitely know you're better off without him.

How to Cut This Sucker Loose

Hanging on to a bad relationship is like trying to save burnt toast. It's ruined and inedible, but you try anyway. You painstakingly scrape off the charred crumbs, hoping to save it but now it's just cold and blotchy...and it's still burnt toast. Don't keep trying to save it. Throw it away and get a new one.

When my ex and I broke up, we were really angry at each other. So I ended up getting together with his best friend and he ended up getting together with one of my friends.

Eight months later, when I moved to San Diego, he begged and begged me to come back. He was starting to show signs that he really loved me. One day he called and said, "If we're gonna work this out, you need to come back now. If you don't, it's over." So I did.

Now this is where it gets a bit twisted.

The friends that we dated ended up dating each other. We moved in with them, and now we were living with the two people we slept with. Obviously this didn't work. And I resented him even more for telling me to come back.

About two months into it, we were having a hard time, of course. Then, I kept noticing this group of club kids (he was a DJ at a local bar) who were coming to the house a lot. He ended up dating one of them while he was still with me! I packed up my stuff—had 800 dollars—and went back to San Diego. I was a mess at that point. The only thing I could do was run.

Getting out was the best thing I ever did.

—"Beth"

If you're being firm with him and he's still contacting you or you find yourself still hanging on, then it's time to go cold turkey. Why? Because both his behavior and yours will cause you to fall into old patterns, spiraling back into playing the "what if" game: What if he just made a mistake?

What if he still has my earrings because he really wants to see me? What if he really wants me back? If you're thinking thoughts like these, then he still has his hooks in you or you keep hooking on to him. Like it or not, you're still emotionally tied to him. Cut him out of your life so you can move forward.

1. Sever all communication. If you didn't do this in the first chapter or you backslid a bit, commit to it now. Unfriend him on Facebook. Block his calls on your phone. Forget where he lives. Avoid his favorite restaurants and hangouts. Remember, we're going cold turkey. Don't slip after a few margaritas and text him at one in the morning saying, "I miss my Pooh Bear." Instead of getting on with your life, you'll be constantly checking your phone for his response. And you'll feel super bad if he doesn't reply at all or sends you a cold, polite message back. Again, by communicating with him you are staying connected to him and prolonging your heartache.

2. Make a list of all your ex's annoying qualities. The more we're in a relationship with someone, the better they look to us. It's these illusions that can keep us emotionally attached. Now that you're out of the tunnel of love, think of all the things that bugged you about him. Get as petty as you want. If it bothered you, write it down. Here are 10 examples of potential annoyances:

1. His beer gut grew two inches every year.

2. He made weird, wailing noises during sex.

3. He was obsessed with *Tosh.0*.

4. He always blamed me for losing his car keys.

5. He chewed his food with his mouth open.

6. He was always flirting with my friends.

7. He left his shaving stubble in the sink.

8. He was rude to everyone.

9. He never cleaned and made beer pyramids in the kitchen.

10. He wore his pants below the waistline with underwear that said, "Spank me."

Refer to this list every time you feel yourself slipping and wanting to contact him.

3. Stay out of his bed. Yep, we're talking sex again. Why? Because maybe you bump into your ex at a restaurant and, damn, he looks good. Next thing you know, you're pressed up against his BMW (I've been there, but it was a Toyota). He kisses you. You let him. He asks you back to his place for dessert. It's so tempting. He's such a hottie, it's hard to resist. But instead of seeing his hotness, you should be seeing that red, hot light flashing telling you to stop right there.

4. Use your friends. When you feel the urge to call your ex, dial a friend instead. Pick a few of your closest girlfriends so if one's not available, you can dial another. If you're feeling particularly vulnerable, you can put them on "red alert," so if your number pops up on their phone they should treat it like an emergency call and pick up right away. These emergency friends will also keep you from doing something stupid like dropping by his favorite bar on a Friday night, stopping by his work to drop off his favorite cappuccino, or leaving your famous macadamia nut cookies on his doorstep (give the cookies to a helpful coworker or one of your friends instead).

The biggest problem with Mr. Flip-Flop is that he's making it more difficult for you to move on and to date other guys. So the next time your ex calls, tell him you don't want to talk to him for a while. Hang up the phone, head out the door, and get on with your life.

Your Emergency Breakup Plan: Ways to Put the Brakes on Breakup Sex

Think first, act second. Think about how you'll feel in the morning after he's left: sad, depressed, and right back where you started.

Work out. Put all that pent-up sexual energy to good use and get a beach-ready body.

Do some shameless flirting. We all want to feel pretty, sexy, and wanted. But getting those feelings from your ex is not the way. Instead, flirt with the cute salesperson at the electronics store, the hot guy who's waiting in line for coffee, or the sexy bartender who makes you a killer apple martini. Whatever. Wherever. A little flirting goes a long way.

(continues)

(continued)

Make out with a new cutie. Again, by having another man desire you, you'll be less likely to try and get that feeling from your ex—but don't sleep with Mr. Cutie. One-night stands can be tricky and can cause you to bond with him before you know whether he's Mr. Right or Mr. Extremely Wrong.

Bottom line: keep your panties on.

He did you a favor because...you will no longer settle for anything less than what you deserve.

The Do-Yourself-a-Favor Workbook: How to Cut the Cord with Your Ex

1. Lie down and close your eyes. Breathe. Relax.

2. Visualize cords that are attached to you on one end and to him on the other (and be honest, there's more than one of them. Find them all).

3. Imagine a pair of scissors cutting those cords, one by one (some may be tougher than others, but I know you can do it).

4. Imagine him drifting away from you and out of your life for good.

5. When he's completely gone, take a deep breath. Exhale, feeling free and clear.

Chapter 8

She Did You A Favor, Too.

Now that you're moving on with your life and letting go of your ex, there's one piece of anger, hurt, or betrayal you may be hanging on to if he cheated on you. That additional hurt lies with Miss Cheater Chick. You see her as the evil witch who stole your guy; she sees you as a barnacle that won't let go. Getting over your ex is hard enough, but getting over the witch who took him from you is another. She's a thorn in your side and it hurts, bad.

Maybe you found out about the affair when you discovered a pair of hoop earrings in the couch that most definitely didn't belong to you; or you saw a bunch of flirtatious emails between him and someone named Sandy; or you got a call from a stranger saying your guy's been shacking up with his wife at the Vagabondage Hotel. Or you just know, because you've been suspecting it for a while and men are terrible liars. You excuse his copious late nights thinking he's working himself to the bone, when really he's banging another babe. She's his neighbor, his coworker, or worse, one of your girlfriends (double skank).

> Women cheat for the same reason they shop, because they can.

It's hard not to be obsessed with the chick who nabbed your guy. Not only are you wounded and sad, you start to think about all the things she is that you're not. You think if you could be more like her you'd be shagging him tonight and she'd be out on the street, throwing pebbles at his window. You spend endless nights filling your head with irrational thoughts and wake up with puffy eyes feeling no better.

> Don't play "what does she have that I don't." It's a losing mind game, because you'll wind up with a whole new set of insecurities.

You Don't Know What You Don't Know

It's easy to view this other woman as some sort of magical temptress who cast a love spell on your guy. But you don't know what really happened and you don't need to know. Just know he's the Cheater Bear who bullshitted his way into her heart and out of yours. So making up crazy scenarios of how it happened, who she is, and how much bigger her boobs are won't do you any good. It'll just keep you in perpetual heartache and damage your self-esteem. It happened, that's it. Don't add to your misery. Stop the obsession and fantasies about how much better she must be to steal your man away. Don't play the victim. And don't waste time sitting around thinking about all the intimate details of their affair, what they're doing now, and if he's telling her the same things he told you when you first dated.

> **Breakup tip:** Adopt a "don't know, don't care" attitude about them. Instead, care about *you*.

I had the unfortunate experience of meeting the "other woman" who my ex cheated with. I couldn't get over how she could look at my pregnant belly and not have a change of heart. I clung to that wounding thought, as well as many others. I became obsessed with how much prettier, smarter, and more adventurous she must be. I held onto those destructive feelings for so long, it killed my self-confidence. I became angry and bitter. I cried all the time. The truth was I didn't know her at all. In my head, I had created a vision of a perfect goddess who had it all together and made myself out to be a worthless piece of nothing. And BTW, years later, he left her, too.

> This isn't a battle you have to win with her; it's a battle you have to win within yourself.

As much as it may seem like it, she's not the enemy. It's useless to get in the ring with her and wrestle for him. This isn't a catfight and he's not a great prize anyway. And don't turn inward and punch the heck out of yourself, either.

This is about healing, not about getting more bruised and beaten down. Again, she doesn't have super sex powers that caught your man, drawing him into her and away from you. She's just a woman. Any woman. And he's just a man— the wrong man for you.

> *I heard a message on my boyfriend's phone from a girl who went on and on about how amazing their trip to Vegas was and how she couldn't stop thinking about it.*
>
> *Unfortunately, that was the time my boyfriend said he was going to the desert by himself because he said he "needed time to think things out."*
>
> —"Janice"

Even though you are unauthorized to obsess about her, I'm still going to go to Who-Is-She Land because let's face it, I know you're going to. We all do it. So let's take a peek at this other chick.

Who Is She Really?

You may say, "Who cares who she is? That witch stole my man!" Yes she did, but just go with this for a second because remember it's all about helping you heal. Let's look at her as a person and not as the Wicked Witch of the West. I'm not saying you two will go for mani-pedis together, but by understanding her more, you'll hurt less. So let's get out of your aching head and see another side.

> *I dated a married man who told me he hadn't had sex with his wife in years and that the marriage was over. I bought it hook, line, and sinker. We met several times a week after work. At first, it was just two people who were attracted to each other meeting for drinks or dinner, pouring our love-starved hearts out to one another. But it escalated to weekly booty calls. Silly me, I equated sex with love. I thought we were going to get married just as soon as he left her. But he never did. One day, he told me his wife was pregnant. My world went into a tailspin. I felt so stupid that I believed all his lies.*
>
> *There's a romantic illusion we mistresses cling to, and we'll buy into it if the guy is a good enough storyteller (and maybe even if he's not) because we just want to believe him so badly.*
>
> —"Hannah"

So who is this other woman? Whether she's a nice girl gone rogue, or the mean girl from high school who turned into an even meaner woman, let's look at some possibilities for her turning from good to super bad. She could be:

* A woman who feels neglected or ignored in her current relationship.

* A woman who's got a sex addiction.

* A woman who's getting back at her boyfriend for cheating on *her*.

* A woman who feels unattractive, unloved, or undesired.

* A woman who's unhappy with herself and is searching for happiness with someone else.

* A bored, desperate housewife who thinks Big Bird is hot.

* A woman who's gullible and believes his lies with all of her heart, despite her intuition.

* A woman who feels underappreciated and is attracted to idiots who cheat on women.

She cheats with him because it makes her feel good in the moment, it fills a void, or it boosts her self-esteem. Her self-respect is in the toilet and she has a desperate need for intimacy.

She doesn't look so super powerful anymore does she?

> You can't steal an honest man, only a dishonest one.

Whatever her reasons for cheating with him, though, it doesn't matter. Her flaws are her problem, and now they're your ex's, too. Is she friend or foe? Neither. She's just someone who's made an unfortunate choice. We've all done that. You're saying no, Pollyanna? Have you ever cheated on a test in school? Cheated on a diet? Told a white lie? Broken something and then secretly put it back? Whether you got away with it or not, think about how you felt. Chances are, you felt pretty bad. But that didn't necessarily make you a bad person. You just made a foolish mistake. Remember, mistakes are lessons. Whatever her reason, she's looking for love, and odds are she found it in the wrong place. It's her loss, not yours.

> **Breakup tip:** By finding compassion you find freedom for yourself.

If this isn't working for you yet, then consider karmic payback. There's no magic time limit on karma. So if it helps, think of it this way: someday, somewhere, when she least expects it, her recklessness will come back to bite her.

Lastly, there are some chicks that get off on stealing other women's men, and yours could fall into that category. It's rare, however, and those relationships usually don't last long, and by then, you will have moved on with a much better man, so she still did you a favor.

The bad part was my boyfriend's ex, Cathy. She had broken up with him to run away with a Parisian restaurateur.

Now, five years later, David was finally in a relationship with someone he loved (me) and Cathy couldn't let that happen. She started by sending cards that I would find around the apartment that would say, "You know we're meant to be together." Then there were phone bills left on the table for me to see. David called her incessantly. My confrontations with him were always met with righteous indignation. Eventually, he started telling me I was "crazy" and "paranoid," so much so that I started to believe it.

(continues)

(continued)

I started doubting myself, and my self-esteem was in the gutter, so I decided to make a change and moved to New York. When I asked David to come with me, he refused. His reasons were weak—something about money, something else about lifestyle. We lived two hours apart and saw each other on weekends. But after six months it became tiresome, so we took a break.

I was finally committed to life in the Big Apple and it was amazing. I made friends and went on dates. About a month later, David reached out to me. We decided to get back together and this time we were going to make it work. This time it was for keeps and we were moving toward marriage. I went home for the weekend to make it official. It felt awkward being with him, but my roots were in my small town with my family. That's where I felt the safest and most settled.

The next morning after David left for work, I started rifling through his drawers. Clearly, there were trust issues. I didn't have to go very far to find what I didn't know I was looking for. In the drawer of his bedside table were three Polaroid pictures of him and Cathy.

Later that night, we met up at a party. I drank a few glasses of wine, pulled him into a hallway, put the promise ring he had bought me into the palm of his hand, and told him it was over. David countered with, "You're drunk. You're crazy. You're going to regret this in the morning." Then he threw the ring at me. I took a bowl of salsa and poured it over his

(continues)

> (continued)
>
> *head. Then, I gasped and said, "Oh my God, I am so drunk and so crazy. I will probably regret that in the morning." That was the last time we ever saw each other.*
>
> *I went on to have a multitude of adventures in Manhattan, Boston, Moscow, Italy, London, and Thailand. Then I met and married the love of my life. We've been married for six years and just had twins. Cathy did me a big favor.*
>
> —"Angie"

How to Give Her Up, Too

By now you've stopped obsessing about your guy; now let's lose the obsession with this chick, as well, because she's getting in the way of your healing. It's time to let go once and for all. Here are some ways to get over her and get on with your life.

1. Don't focus on her. Remember, by putting her up on a pedestal, intentionally or not, you are keeping yourself in emotional quicksand. The truth is, if he didn't cheat with her, he would've cheated with someone else. So here's what you do:

✱ Don't talk about her.

✱ Don't Google her.

✱ If you accidently bump into her at your nail salon, look away (and maybe find another salon to go to).

* Every time you start to think of her, think of a fluffy bunny instead.

* Think about how great *you* are.

* Think about the hot men you're gonna meet next, while she's stuck with Mr. Hot Mess.

2. Don't hate her. I know this is a tough one. But remember, you cannot steal an honest man, only a dishonest one.

So whenever a hateful thought about her pops into your head, replace it with a loving thought about yourself, even if you sometimes want to rip her lungs out. Remember, hate is toxic to *you*. It's like taking poison and expecting the other person to die. Don't have a bitch session about her thinking it will make you feel better. What we focus on can stress us out, put pressure on our bodies, and possibly make us sick. It's just like trashing your ex in public—it only keeps this person very present in your thoughts and gives her power she doesn't deserve.

Don't hate her; love you.

3. Don't compete with her. When something like this happens, it's hard not to feel competitive and get your cat claws out. Her actions made you feel betrayed, hurt, or humiliated. Your instinct may be to fight back. This woman will never be your friend, but you don't need to make her your enemy either. She really has nothing to do with you. Instead, focus on all the awesome women in your life who love and support you.

> *I went through a terrible divorce. My husband was scared he was going to lose a bunch of money in the settlement, so he used every tactic to break me down. What made it worse was the woman he was having an affair with got into it, as well. She would email me nasty messages, confront me, and would say bad things about me to friends. It was awful. I was so beaten down by this bully, I cried all the time.*
>
> *Finally, a friend gave me the best advice. She told me to disconnect from this woman—don't look at her, don't talk to her, and don't trash talk back. The moment I started doing that, I felt so much more empowered and was finally able to get my life on track. I got my lawyer involved and he helped monitor our emails. Eventually, I won the settlement in the divorce, as well. And I met a new guy who I'm completely in love with and am happier than I've ever been.*
>
> —"Suzanne"

As much as it may feel like it, you are *not* in competition with her. Don't feel like you've lost and she's won. Remember, it's actually her loss and your gain.

> You are not competing with her. In fact you've already won. You've won your freedom.

SHE DID YOU A FAVOR, TOO.

4. Don't change because of her. This is not the time to get a radical new haircut, a nose job, or to take up roller-blading (unless you really want to learn how) because you're trying to be like her and win your ex back—and at this point, why would you still want to? You'll have to wait for that radical haircut to grow out, that nose job could wreck your beautiful face, and rollerblading could give you a broken ankle to go with your broken heart. Again, you're idealizing her way too much, trying to be what you think your ex wants, and most importantly not being yourself.

5. Practice forgiveness. I know you're not in the mood to forgive her. I get it. I say *practice* because this is a process of healing—you're not going to get there in one night, and you may not completely get there. It doesn't matter. Your thoughts will be more optimistic and it'll be easier to keep moving forward.

> *After my husband's affair, I made a choice that I was going to live my life better than I had ever lived it before. So this "other woman" ended up being a catalyst, because the affair freed me to move into the life I came here to live.*
>
> —"Nina"

If you can find the gratitude in this situation, it will further help you to let go. Because this isn't about her, it's about you. The truth is, she spared you from a relationship that wasn't meant to be. She didn't steal him from you. He wasn't a good bargain to begin with. She also opened the door for a new man to come through—one who you truly deserve. For that, you can be thankful (without giving her a box of chocolates).

10 Reasons She Did You a Favor

1. She's stuck with Mr. Cheater Pants and all his emotional baggage.

2. She has to put up with his mood swings, his messes, or his poorly shaped mustache.

3. You're no longer with a guy you don't trust (and she won't be able to trust him either).

4. She's helped you learn compassion; once you get over the feeling you want to put her head through a wall.

5. He'll probably leave her, too.

6. You're out of a relationship that clearly wasn't right for you.

7. Time is a precious commodity and he's not wasting yours anymore. So she saved you wasted time.

8. Ready or not, you were done with him already.

9. This situation is helping you refocus on all the reasons you kick ass.

10. She's given you the opportunity to find a man worthy of your time and love.

The truth is, this too shall pass. This breakup is helping you grow into a compassionate, super woman. So focus on you. Turn your thoughts to how fabulous you are and how lucky you are to be free of him. You may even run into her someday and say, "Thank you." You never know.

> **She did you a favor because...this breakup is helping you to recognize your own power.**

The Do-Yourself-a-Favor Workbook: Your Awesome Self-Esteem Booster

1. Send an email to your closest friends, asking them what they think is great about you (if you're uncomfortable with this, say it's an exercise I told you to do).

2. Receive the love-fest that follows.

3. Compile a list of your favorites. Look at them often (tape them to your mirror, your refrigerator, or your forehead if you have to). Believe every awesome word!

Part III

Moving On To Your Super Fab Life

Chapter 9

He Did You a Favor because It's Time to Get a Life, Cinderella.

Now it's time to focus on your fabulous self and to get rid of any blocks, so you can keep moving forward in a more powerful way. With that in mind, let's look at any limiting beliefs that may be preventing you from fully stepping into your awesomeness.

Answer these questions: Do you use love as an excuse to stay stuck? Would you gladly trade your high heels for a pair of glass slippers? Do you believe that life will be better once you find The One?

Then you could be trapped in the Cinderella mindset. Deep down, you may think no matter how bad things get in your life, eventually your prince will come along and you'll get your happily-ever-after. But the Cinderella fairy tale sets us up for disappointment and failure when it doesn't work out exactly the way we expect.

> Cinderella is not living her best life right now; she is waiting for a man to give her a better life.

What Does Princess Cinderella Do When Things Go Terribly Wrong?

Sometimes Cinderella clings to the prince, still believing they're destined to be together. Or she'll put up with his belittling, believing (being the nice girl that she is) that if she shows enough kindness, eventually he'll change his bad behavior. Or she'll allow his frequent business trips, telling herself that he's working hard, even though her intuition tells her there's something else going on. Or she'll be bored and directionless, puttering around his castle, attending to his needs and abandoning her own.

I dated my prince during the height of my Cinderella years. When we met, he had great friends; I had toxic friends. He was rich; I was struggling to get out of debt. He was successful; I was still trying to get my career off the ground. After we married, I had the ideal life every girl dreams of on the outside—a beautiful home, money, friends, and I was a creative partner in his projects. But on the inside, my self-confidence and self-worth were dying a slow and painful death. Before long, insecurity and need ruled my life. I fell deep into the Cinderella trap, depending on him for everything, including my happiness. Every year it got progressively worse; I retreated into his life more and more and lost sight of my own. My fairy tale spun upside down, ending in the tragic death of the relationship and of my self-image. The dream I longed for and achieved was gone for good and I was crushed beyond belief. I had lost my way in the forest and didn't know how to get out.

The Princess in You

Who is this fairy tale woman we all try to emulate? The modern day Cinderella may be hard to spot, because she's not stuck at home sweeping ashes out of the fireplace. And she's not lounging on the couch all day eating cake and binge watching "Once Upon A Time." Here are some women who may be stuck in the Cinderella mindset:

* She's got a job, although she hates it, but it's fine because eventually some rich dude is going to come along and wipe out her debts—and *then* she can quit.

* She constantly feels underappreciated at work or at home, but she's a "good girl" so she doesn't say anything or do anything about it.

* She's a CinderMama who does everything for her family (even though they are capable of doing a lot for themselves). She's exhausted all the time, believing she has to "do it all."

* She's a successful workingwoman, but when her husband's out of town, she feels incredibly alone and can't sleep until he comes back.

* She's pursuing her dreams, but probably not as purposefully as she should, knowing one day her prince will come along, they'll get married, and then she can go for her dreams comfortably and safely.

* She's too focused on making others happy, and not focused enough on making herself happy.

Additionally, some Cinderellas start off as strong, independent women; but fall into the fairy tale trap when they get into a relationship and need and dependence sets in. Before they know it, they're relying on others for their happiness instead of creating it themselves.

I have a Cinderella-minded friend who's a successful real estate agent in her forties. She's been divorced for years and is struggling with the second act of her life. One day she said to me, "I just want to find a man who'll take care of me." Since then, she's spent a ton of time online dating. The problem is that with every date she sets her expectations way too high. Also, she's ready to write him off at the slightest slip-up, like if his name is Arnold and he orders an Arnold Palmer (maybe he just likes them). This woman is beautiful and smart, yet she's still looking for the perfect man to take care of her.

Which Princess Do You Relate To?

In *The Wizard of Oz*, Glinda asks Dorothy, "Are you a good witch or a bad witch?" Like witches, there are good and bad princesses. So which princess are you? Let's look at three types:

The Needy Princess

She's a princess whose ultimate desire is to be taken care of. She thinks if she can find a successful man, then her life will be much better. This princess is waiting for someone else to make all her dreams come true.

✳ She depends on others for her happiness.

* She's insecure.

* She has a conscious or unconscious fear of independence.

* She craves attention.

* She cares deeply about what other people think.

This princess is looking outside for her happiness, instead of finding it within herself and thus attracting her ideal mate.

Additionally, putting pressure on a man to take care of all our needs and desires leads to bitterness and resentment. Some women are taught to believe they're nothing without a man. But nothing gets you a whole lot more of nothing. If you enter a relationship being needy and insecure, be prepared for him to treat you like a doormat or dump you when he gets angry or bored.

If you are unhappy with yourself, princess, landing a prince will not make you happier. You'll drag him down and eventually he will leave.

The Stubborn Princess

An independent princess is much more alluring to our modern day prince, but let's not go to the extreme either. These days, women are more immersed in the work force, giving up their fuzzy slippers for high heels. Being a working woman is fabulous, but some women end up becoming so fiercely independent that they become inflexible in relationships.

* She's extremely set in her ways.

* She always has to be right.

* She's super high-maintenance.

* She's critical of others.

* She's controlling and manipulative.

Here's another thing about the Stubborn Princess—she has to do everything herself or have everything her way. This'll also cause your prince to jump ship.

Be independent, but don't emasculate him. Men still need to provide for and cherish women. Women need to receive and be cherished. Don't take that away. Let him open your car door, pick up the dinner check, or get your car detailed. Chivalry is definitely not dead, sister. Allow him to do things for you.

The lesson? Don't be so self-righteous and set in your ways that you don't leave room for a man in your life.

The Warrior Princess

This is the princess who every guy wants to capture. She's authentic and ambitious. She's kind and loving. She's open to new experiences and takes risks. She receives help when she needs it, but isn't dependent on anyone. She listens to guidance, but is free to choose what's best for her.

* She's self-assured.

* She's independent.

* She gives and receives love equally.

* She's courageous and kind.

* She values her self-worth.

This princess knows what she wants and goes for it. She's not looking for happiness in a man, but has the strength to find it within. She's a great partner in relationships. She's also surrounded by friends who mirror back the confident, loving woman she is.

Additionally, a Warrior Princess will have the strength to walk away from a bad or abusive relationship. It takes courage to let go.

Now which princess do you want to be?

Get Ready To Rock, Princess Awesome

By recognizing and acknowledging your Cinderella tendencies after your breakup, you can turn them around, change any self-limiting beliefs, and redefine your life. Sure, it may be scary at times. Those unfamiliar woods can be pretty dark and frightening, but I did it and it was liberating. I broke free, reclaiming my life and career. Only then did I fully realize how much my ex-prince did me a favor.

Now, it's your turn. Here are three great ways to go from Princess Cinderella to Warrior Princess:

1. Lower expectations of others and expect more from you. Start by looking more realistically at who you are and what you *really* want. Remember, the key to your happiness lies within and not with others.

2. Stop believing in the "love will conquer all" myth and begin conquering your own life. Let go of any self-limiting beliefs and get moving toward accomplishing your own dreams. Don't let anything discourage you from doing something great. Take baby steps every day to get you closer and closer to what you desire. Get busy, turn your life around, and step into success.

3. Do more for you. Remember, our love and value has to come from within. So always take time out for some tender lovin' self-care. Do whatever nourishes and replenishes you (take a power nap, read a self-help blog, or go for a run). By taking care of *you* first, you'll be happier, more balanced, *and* have more love to give to others.

> **Favorable tip:** Your true joy and happiness have nothing to do with circumstances. They are entirely up to you and what you create.

Live Your Fairy Tale Life Now

Does this mean you shouldn't dress up and run the princess marathon at Disneyland? Or you should ditch your Barbie Dream House? Or give up on the idea of true love? No. Dream on. Just remember to find your happiness within, keep an open heart, and be willing to kiss some frogs to get there if you have to. It's all about the journey.

When you're ready to date again, let a man to treat you like a princess, but be a self-assured one. By treasuring your self-worth, you can decide if you want to invite this new dude into your castle, or not. And if he suddenly turns into an evil ogre, close the door on that sucker and change the locks. Lift the drawbridge and let him fall in the moat, because he's not doing you any good.

Always remember that the relationships you choose are reflections of yourself. Healthy, independent women attract healthy men. Unhealthy, needy women attract unhealthy men. Don't forget, by building a better relationship with you, you will attract better relationships with others. If I were still that needy, insecure princess of years ago, would I have attracted the amazing man I'm in a relationship with now? No. In fact, some of things that attracted him in the first place were my courage, independence, and creativity. Things I had abandoned in my previous relationship.

So get clear, get active, and get out there Miss Awesome. Be optimistic, knowing your possibilities are endless. You *can* have your cake and eat it too. Believe in yourself. Pursue your passions. Create a new fairy tale—one where Cinderella gets the dream life she wants *and* gets her prince.

The truth is, there are a lot of princes riding around in the forest. If you honor yourself and keep your heart open, they'll find you. In the meantime, you'll be rockin' that tiara all by your fabulous self.

> **He did you a favor because...now you have the great opportunity to live a fairy tale life and land a much better prince!**

The Do-Yourself-a-Favor Workbook: Your Princess Test

Which Princess Are You?

1. The Princess you most identify with is:

    A. Cinderella.

    B. Princess Leia.

    C. You actually identify more with Maleficent.

2. What are a princess's most important qualities?

    A. Being beautiful, a great shopper, and willing to set aside what she wants to please her man.

    B. Confidence, courage, and kindness.

    C. The ability to boss around well-trained assistants who are at her beck and call 24 hours a day—hey, it's a gift.

3. What's the best way for a princess to get what she wants?

    A. Beg and throw a tantrum; since she's devoted her life to the prince, he needs to give back once in a while.

    B. Ask and be willing to receive.

    C. Be demanding; ultimatums trump requests.

4. The man of your dreams is a guy who'll:

    A. Take care of all your needs and solve your problems.

    B. Respect and appreciate you for who you are and be a loving partner.

C. Put you on a pedestal and do whatever you want, whenever you want.

5. You're lost in the woods. You...

   A. Sit and wait. Someone will eventually come along and help you.

   B. Look for your path and ask for directions. When you find it, you walk it with renewed confidence.

   C. Tell the first person you see to go find the path for you; you're much too busy right now to deal with this yourself.

6. Your potential prince asks you out on a date, but he's an hour late. You:

   A. Sit there and wait. Whenever he shows up is fine with you. You're just happy he asked you out.

   B. Call and ask, "What's up?"

   * If he's lost, or he's stuck in major traffic, or he had to take his parakeet to the hospital, you give him a break.

   * If he's calling from home saying he overslept, or was talking with a friend and lost track of time, then suggest you go out another night—or not. Your choice. Then you hang up and dial up some friends for dinner.

   C. Leave him a nasty note and go clubbing with your friends.

7. You're living with your prince and he's incredibly messy. You:

   A. Make excuses that he's "really busy" or "that's just the way he is" and clean up after him.

   B. You lightly remind him to pick up his stuff. You suggest a beer and pizza cleaning party once a week where you clean up together. If he still expects you to clean up after him, remind him that you're his girlfriend, not his maid.

   C. Throw his stuff on the lawn in the pouring rain. He'll get the idea.

8. Your prince has turned into a frog. You:

   A. Keep dating him. If you kiss him sweetly enough, he'll turn back into a prince.

   B. Put him back in the pond and go fishing.

   C. Take that frog down and make him pay until he croaks.

9. Your Fairy Godmother grants you one wish. It is:

   A. To send you a wealthy prince who'll make all your dreams come true.

   B. To find a man who loves you unconditionally and supports your career.

   C. To send you a prince who will obey your every command!

Your Princess Answers:

Mostly A's:

Poor Cinderella—you are scrubbing floors and putting your prince up on a pedestal. Fill your drinking goblet up with courage and self-compassion. Think about what makes *you* happy and do it often.

Mostly B's:

You are a Warrior Princess who is worthy of her crown and takes on life with confidence. Good for you! Keep it up!

Mostly C's:

Take a chill pill Miss Uptight, and let's get some perspective here. If you keep this up, you'll not only lose any prince who might be waiting in the wings, you'll lose your friends as well.

The Do-Yourself-a-Favor Workbook: Your Princess Makeover

Your Magic Toolkit:

* Practice self-compassion, every day.

* Find your purpose and do it—this is where your power is, princess.

* Smile...a lot. It instantly boosts your mood and your attractiveness.

* Value your self-worth and compare yourself to no one. Hey, there's only one of you out there.

* Be fearless and take chances—you never know what great opportunities are waiting for you.

Get Yourself a Fairy Godmother:

This could be a mentor, a coach, or even a great friend you look up to, to help you make the transition from fearful to fabulous. Choose someone you trust and who really gets you. This person will be there to remind you how outstanding and courageous you really are.

My fairy godmother was my amazing life coach. I wouldn't be the person I am today without her incredible guidance.

Acknowledge what's great about you and be the power princess you're meant to be!

Chapter 10

He Did You a Favor because Forgiving Him Gives You a Better You.

Now that you're taking back your power and feeling better, it's time for the final hurdle—forgiveness. Why forgive? Because by forgiving him, you free yourself. Forgiveness is about loving you enough to let this relationship go. This isn't about calling up your ex and saying, "I forgive you." You don't have to. Remember, this is about taking care of your emotional health, not his. So here's where you start...

Get Rid of Anger Once and for All

Before you can forgive him, it's crucial to let go of any residual anger you may have. Is he a D-bag for sending you a breakup text? Yes. Is he a big jerk for cheating on you? Yep. Is he an idiot for lying to you? Uh-huh. But here's the thing, do you want to be happy, or right? By not forgiving him for his jerky acts, you're prolonging the pain. Holding on to resentment, rage, or bitterness towards him is like having him live rent-free in your head. It's like he's cluttering up your bedroom and monopolizing the bathroom. Forgiveness clears the space and gives you room to lead a happier life. So if you haven't released all your rage towards him in the first chapter, give yourself 24 hours. Go at it like a 20-mile run. Beat the crap out of a pillow, yell, do your best anger dance, whatever it takes to get it all out. Yeah, he did a sucky thing to you, but wallowing in bitterness will get you another dateless, sex-less night with a chick flick and gobs of Reese's Peanut Butter Cups. It'll make you spiral into an "all men suck" attitude, which will keep you perpetually alone in a house full of cats, knitting a scarf you'll never wear.

While you're doing your 24-hour anger dance, don't suddenly feel like you have to send him an email detailing all the shitty things he said or did, like telling you to lose weight, or not listening to you, or picking his teeth in public. You've come so far, do you really want to go back into the trenches with Mr. Heartbreaker, or be the better woman? If you still feel the need to write your angry thoughts down, then pull out a notebook, put on some heartbreaker music, and go to town. Get it all out. When you're done, let go.

> *When I started doing work on myself I thought, "Who am I carrying resentment for?" My ex and my father. Then I asked myself, "What do I resent them for? What is my responsibility in this? How can I heal this? And in what ways did it help me?" I finally understood it was all about anger and abuse. After I answered those questions, the final part was to let go.*
>
> *—"Beth"*

The best way to come out a winner is not by torturing yourself with thoughts and actions against him, but by forgiving him and setting yourself free so you can find real love. This is why forgiveness is so powerful.

> After my breakup, I wasn't going to bypass all my anger and hurt. I allowed myself to feel everything I was feeling. I kept practicing self-forgiveness and forgiveness of him. It's an ongoing process. I may be forgiving him for years, but I feel lighter and lighter. I don't think there's any way to move on without forgiveness.
>
> —"Sheryl"

It took me a while to forgive, but here's what I did. I practiced letting go of any negative thoughts that were still attached to my past relationship. When a negative thought came up, I'd say to myself, "Stop," and kick it right out of my head. Then I'd replace it with something like, "I'm amazing and I deserve an amazing guy." I kept doing this over and over, until my negative thoughts diminished.

So have you gotten out all your anger and resentment? Have you let go of all your negative thoughts and words? Okay, good for you! You're ready. Here are some tips for forgiving his sorry ass and moving on with your great life.

Be Willing to Forgive

The first step is simply to be willing to forgive. If you're still reluctant you won't get there. You don't have to push or force it. Just like healing your broken heart, it takes time. And who knows what the catalyst will be. It could be that you see your ex in a new light and he loses his charm and appeal. Or your ex cheats again with someone else and you realize it's a pattern with him. Or you date a new hottie. It doesn't matter. What matters is that you get there. At some point, you will go from being in it, to so over it. That's when you can learn to make peace with him and yourself.

Find Compassion for Mr. Heartbreaker

Compassion is the best way to forgive. If it helps, look at him as a bad child who didn't know any better. For him to do what he did to you, he may have been broken in some way. Or he's got a lot to learn about how to be good in a relationship. Or maybe he feels bad right now and doesn't like himself all that much because of the shitty way he treated you.

> *I totally had an existential moment through forgiving this bully guy I dated.*
>
> *When he broke up with me, he pulled the big, bully move—he used some very personal information I gave him. He turned it around, threw it in my face, and made fun of me for it. He went to a place that nobody goes. I got so mad, I started making myself literally sick.*
>
> (continues)

(continued)

At that point, I thought, "I have two choices: I can get in the ring with him and make him feel as bad as he made me feel, or I can forgive him." Deep down, I knew I only had one choice. Getting into the ring with him was not an option because, first of all, I didn't want to be as disgusting and mean as him, and second of all I wasn't as good at it. So I meditated for a full day on it. I just kept thinking and basically went to this place of just finding compassion for him. I realized that anybody who could hurt someone the way he hurt me has to hate himself on such a grand scale. Nobody who loves himself lashes out like that. In that, I found true compassion for him.

A year later, I went to Burning Man. Through mutual friends, we ended up being in the same camp. I actually didn't really care. That's when I knew I was really over him. It was no big deal.

As it turned out, I met this guy there and we ended up having the most incredible romantic time. It was such poetic justice. I mean, I felt I was given this gift of forgiving my ex. Every time I had a fun, sexy moment with this new guy, my ex was watching. Had I still cared, it would've been the greatest revenge ever. But I really didn't care, because I had forgiven him.

—"Patricia"

Letting go is about releasing your attachment to him. It's not about being weak or admitting defeat. Instead, it can help you to lose any emotional baggage once and for all. Pack it up and send it off on a one-way ticket so you're free and clear.

> *My husband had an affair, but it ended. We tried to work it out, but one morning I woke up and thought, "I am complete." I went into the kitchen and said it to him. That was it. We began our physical separation and eventual divorce. I knew I didn't want to be with this man anymore. I couldn't forget what he did, but I could forgive. I knew this was the key to my liberation and that I was ready to let go. Also, I knew my life was going to be better, because I had the opportunity to take the time and sink into myself, to find out who I was, and to find someone who could really fulfill me.*
>
> *—"Vicky"*

Forgive Yourself

It's so easy to judge ourselves for how we acted in a relationship and blame ourselves for it ending. But remember, this self-flagellation does you no good either. Don't forget, for all the things you think you did wrong in this relationship, your actions served a purpose—to help you learn and grow. You didn't do anything "bad" or "wrong." The truth is, you did the best you could.

Knowing all that I know now, would I have done it differently with my ex-husband? Sure. But it doesn't matter. I had to go through what I did to learn the lessons I needed to learn. No one's perfect. By telling yourself you did your best at that time, you free yourself from beating down your self-esteem with a two-by-four.

Here are some things you can forgive yourself for:

1. **Being too clingy in the relationship.** You are learning that having independence will help keep your sense of self.

2. **Losing your self-esteem.** You are learning to believe in yourself.

3. **Giving up your friends to be with him.** You are learning how important it is to keep your own identity when you're in a relationship.

4. **Allowing him to belittle you.** You are learning to respect yourself.

5. **Getting so caught up in his needs that you lost sight of your own.** You are learning that your needs are important as well.

6. **Not communicating.** You are learning to speak up for what you want.

7. **Doubting yourself.** You are learning to value yourself and your opinions.

8. **Not taking better care of yourself.** You are learning to put your needs first.

9. **Taking his abusiveness.** This is the wrong relationship and you're lucky to be out of it. Don't repeat this

pattern with another. You are learning to stand up for yourself.

10. Letting the relationship drag on when you knew it wasn't working. Enough said!

Here's something else to remember: If you want to attract love in another man, you have to love yourself first and that means forgiving yourself.

Forgive His Friends and Yours

Maybe you're harboring some anger towards his or your friends. Maybe they knew he was unhappy, or that he going to break up with you, or they knew he was schtupping his boss and they did nothing about it. Don't waste time blaming them either. They were between a rock and a hard place. It wasn't their decision for him to break up with you. Nothing they could've done or said would've tipped it either way. Instead, they were standing on the sidelines watching this losing game go into agonizing overtime. Give them a break. They may or may not have made the best decisions, but it's really not about them anyway. Again, by blaming them you're putting time and energy into the wrong place.

> **Favorable tip:** By letting go of the past, you are empowering yourself to live a happier life.

While we're in forgiving mode, how about forgiving everyone who's ever wronged you?

How to Forgive Everywhere in Your Life

Forgive the crazy driver who cut you off, the grocery bagger who forgot to put the Snickers bar in your bag, or your parents for not encouraging you enough. The truth is, that crazy driver could've had an emergency; that grocery bagger could be nervous because it's his first day on the job; and your parents, well that's something else altogether, but for now let's just say they did the best they could with what they grew up with and how they were raised.

By forgiving, you're losing all that emotional junk food so you can have a svelte, beautiful, healthier you!

> **He did you a favor because...you've lost that emotional weight and are free to live a healthier, happier life.**

The Do-Yourself-a-Favor Workbook: Your Emotional Cleanse

If you want to get emotional freedom to forgive, you can. First, let's clear out your emotional fridge. Get rid of any bitter, rotten feelings that are eating away at you. We're clearing out these spoiled feelings to get your emotions back in balance. To start:

* Purge any rotten feelings about this breakup. You don't keep expired food for 6 months, so why keep bad feelings around? This relationship is past its expiration date, so let it go.

* Discard any self-loathing, because really, who is it helping?

* Dump out any hurt that is blocking your flow of happiness, because being stuck in misery sucks, big time.

Now that you've cleaned out all the bad stuff, you can start your emotional cleanse with...

Breakfast—*Revitalize with a Healthy, Emotional Breakfast:*

"Awesome Renew Smoothie"

* A cup of self-love: As soon as you wake up put your hand on your heart like it's a newborn baby.

* A big helping of passion and purpose: Feel the heart of who you are and know you are meant to share this gift with others.

* A handful of confidence: Say three times out loud, "I am confident and I can accomplish anything."

Lunch—*Fill Up On:*

* A nutritious, healthy bowl of reasons you're awesome.

* Add a side of why you're happy he's gone.

* Toss in a bunch of clarity on why your relationship ended and how you'll do certain things differently next time.

* Top it off with trust that a much better man is out there for you.

Dinner—*Have a Nourishing Meal Consisting Of:*

* A cup of gratitude for all the excellent things in your life.

* A bunch of appreciation for your loving friends.

* A big helping of optimism for the future.

And hydrate every day with self-compassion. The more you do this the more quickly the emotional toxins will leave your mind and body.

Unlike most cleanses; you can do this as often as you like, for as long as you like. By filling up on these good emotional calories first, you'll be full and there will be no room left for the fattening, bad emotional calories.

If you slip and eat up a day in anger, fear, or resentment, don't beat yourself up. Just go back to your healthy emotional food plan the next day. Sometimes it takes a bit for your emotions to catch up with your thoughts, but give it time and you'll get there.

Chapter 11

He Did You a Favor because Your Ex-Boyfriend May Be a Better Friend.

𝒴ou're finally getting back on track with your life and you get a call from him asking, "Can we still be friends?" The real question is, is there a place for him in your new life or are you making a super bad choice by having him around? Let's get serious and find out if this is really right for you. Here's where you get to decide whether he's got friend potential or if you should just file him away in your Ex-Files for good.

Can You Be Friends?

You may say, "Sure, we can be friends." Are you absolutely certain? Because this is the same as, "Sure, I can handle you calling me to talk about your problems," or "Sure, I want to hear about the office party you went to," or "It's good you went on a date." Did you flinch? Then hold off on jumping into the friend zone with your ex. That was the litmus test to see if you can hear him talk about a great party he went to or his dating life without wanting to punch something.

If you choose to be friends with him because you still miss him and need him to be a part of your life, think again. I've jumped into the friend shark tank too soon with some of my exes and got bitten badly. It always came down to the same thing: I was still emotionally attached. I wanted his affection and attention any way I could get it.

Are You Doing Yourself a Favor by Being Friends with Him?

Give yourself time to consider this one. Just because he wants to be friends now, doesn't mean you have to say yes. You need to decide if you can handle it or if it's going to send you back to the kitchen floor with a bag of Pepperidge Farm cookies.

If you can't be friends with him right now, it doesn't mean that you can't be friends in the future. Time will give you confidence. Time will give you new relationships. Time will give you a clear head to make the right decision for you. Time really does heal all wounds. So take as long as you need. There is no wrong answer here, just be honest with yourself and do what's best for you.

> **Breakup tip:** Time is your friend when he can't be.

If you didn't pass the friends litmus test, then don't re-friend him on Facebook, don't read his emails, and don't return his calls. You're not ready, and that's okay. Don't fool yourself. Don't torture yourself. You still need time. How much time? Time enough for you to heal the hurt, move on with your life, and start dating again. Part of that healing is replacing that space he used to take up in you by filling that void with something, or even someone, else. Most importantly, don't rush it. Don't jump in before your heart is fully healed, otherwise that wound's going to open up all over again. You've come too far to let that happen.

The Top 10 Reasons You Cannot Be Friends

1. You still get butterflies whenever he texts you.

2. You're still checking his Facebook page to find out what he's up to.

3. You still fantasize about having sex with him.

4. You're thinking more about him and less about yourself.

5. You're still showing up at places you think he'll be.

6. You're still watching cheesy romantic movies at one in the morning and substituting yourself and him for the lead characters.

(continues)

(continued)

7. You spot a bridal shop and fantasize what it would be like to marry him.

8. You're having trouble concentrating in your job because you can't stop thinking about all the great times you had together.

9. He calls you and you have to comfort yourself with a cheeseburger and fries.

10. You went on a date (good for you!), but then called your ex to trash the guy in hopes that your ex would take you back.

If any of the above are true, you've still got feelings for your ex. It may be obvious, but it has to be said. We all play Jedi mind tricks with ourselves. You could be denying the one thing that's keeping you stuck where you are. He's not your friend if you cry after you get off the phone with him, or you get that old familiar feeling and can't shake it for days, or you feel sick because he just told you he's moving to Florida. Don't kid yourself when it comes to your feelings—they're your best navigator and will honestly tell you if you're ready or not.

The bottom line is, don't let your ego get in the way. Don't pretend you're okay with being friends to save face when you really want to claw your (or his) eyes out.

> *It's crazy the stupid, humiliating things we do to pretend to be friends and to be okay with it.*
>
> *In college, I was madly in love with my boyfriend...and then he started dating one of my best friends. I was trying to be cool about it so he wouldn't see how much I was hurting. I didn't want him to have the satisfaction of knowing he broke my heart. So, just in case my heart wasn't being run over enough, I had the two of them over for dinner, thinking it would save my pride. It was pure ego. It ended up being the worst, most heartbreaking night of my life.*
>
> —"Anne"

Why Friends-with-Benefits Never Works

If you're considering shagging your ex, you're not ready to be friends. Or you may have already had a moment of weakness (or two...or three...) and had breakup sex. Remember, as great as this sounds in theory, it's not a good idea. You may think this will help your heart, but even if you have the best orgasm of your life, it'll ultimately make everything worse. Remember oxytocin? It'll bind you emotionally to him and give you more heartache. And what if he gets dressed and bolts right after? Or what if he gets a text from another woman when he's still in bed with you? Or what if he told you after several booty calls that he didn't want to sleep with you anymore? How would you feel?

> *For a while after we broke up, we were still having sex. This was something we were really good at it. Then I found out he was dating someone else and I left. We didn't speak for five years.*
>
> *One day, he contacted me. When we went out, all those old feelings came back. For years after, we had sex on and off, but we never tried to get back together. I would have, but he wouldn't. It made me feel like I was never really good enough to date, but I was good enough to have sex with. Finally, I couldn't do it anymore.*
>
> —"Carrie"

If you give in to him you're not honoring yourself. You're just getting a quick fix from someone you're still crushing on who can't commit. He's asking for a casual hookup, not a meaningful relationship. A guy friend of mine said, "Men will always take friends-with-benefits, because it's like winning the lottery."

Additionally, you're keeping one foot (or in this case your whole body) in the past, instead of moving on to someone new. I know. I've been there. I've had my share of friend-sex. It was great sex, but I always ended up getting hurt in the end. Looking back, it wasn't worth the emotional toll it took on my heart.

> Friends-with-benefits is like going on a shopping spree and buying 10 pairs of shoes, but feeling horrible when you get the bill later.

How to Make the Break

If you realize you can never be friends, it's okay. Remember, you had your time with him for a reason and now that time is over. It's hard sometimes because this guy was an important part of your life. This doesn't mean you don't have feelings for him or think of him, it just means he's not adding anything to your life anymore. By letting him go, you're freeing yourself up for new friends and relationships—ones that will enrich your life, not deplete it.

So now that you're clear you can't be friends, here are some tips to help you make a clean break:

* Think of all the reasons the relationship didn't work.

* Think of the qualities that bugged you about him.

* Think about how you would feel if you saw him sucking face with someone else (how it would be like putting your heart through a meat grinder).

You are now a professional athlete who's training for the "I don't need him anymore" marathon. Get in the zone. Keep moving toward your goal so you can reach the finish line. Keep being honest and taking care of yourself.

You still can't break free of him? Or you feel yourself backsliding? Ask your friends to remind you why it's not a good idea to be friends with him (I'm sure they can come up with a laundry list) and have them help you stick to it. You want to call him about your promotion? You want to text him a pic of your new puppy? You want to tell him you watched the entire series of *Game of Thrones* in two days? Call your friends—your real friends.

When He Won't Take No for an Answer.

If he takes your, "No" as a, "Maybe," and keeps trying to push the friendship option, stand your ground. I've had that happen, too. He thinks if he still likes you, why can't you both just hang out? Or be Facebook pals? Or go to for coffee every once in a while? If you decide you can't be friends right now, dig in and refuse to budge. If he really cares about you, he'll respect your decision. If not, he's not a friend and never will be.

> *Greg and I had been dating for six months and our chemistry was ridiculous. We couldn't spend two minutes in a room together without wanting to jump each other's bones. One day, I got the dreaded, "I just want to be friends" call. I was devastated. I knew deep down I couldn't do it.*
>
> *He didn't give up, though. He kept calling and wanting to see me. This went on for months. Finally, I gave in. Then we started having sex again, only now I wasn't staying over for breakfast, I was leaving in the middle of the night and waking up in my bed the next morning, feeling awful. Still, each time he called and asked me out, I said, "Yes." Secretly, I thought maybe we could still end up together.*
>
> *Finally, I realized I was just dragging out the pain. I stopped returning his calls and cut him out of my life for good.*
>
> *—"Joanna"*

When You Want to Be Friends, but He Doesn't

Maybe you feel you can be friends, but he says he can't. I know it hurts like hell just like your breakup did, but he may want to close that chapter of his life for one reason or another. It doesn't matter what the reason is, and you shouldn't go digging for the answer. He's made himself clear and you should be grateful he's not stringing you along. He's doing you a favor. Now you can get closure, too.

When Friendship Is an Option

If you've taken the litmus test and passed with flying colors, then you could be ready to be friends. Just make sure it doesn't hold you back from your own growth or from meeting a new guy. Double check to make sure all those emotional cords attached to your ex have been severed and you're completely healed.

Additionally, if you feel you can be friends, then you have to be willing to reestablish a new type of relationship and accept that it won't be like it was before. He's never going to be your BFF because, let's face it, you've seen each other naked. But you can cultivate a friendship that is good and healthy for both of you, if you're willing to approach it in a fresh way. Develop an "out with the old, in with the new" attitude.

Being friends with my ex-husband took time. What made it harder was that I had a lot of emotional scarring.

What made it easier was that we'd been great friends before we dated, so I chose to focus on that. It was a challenge, but I wanted to try for the sake of our daughter. The moment I knew we could be friends was when I realized I wasn't in love him anymore, but I still liked him a lot. Only then could I make the right choice for me, and stick to it. It took a while, but I just kept focusing on the positive aspects of our friendship. Now, years later, we're better friends and co-parents than we ever were as husband and wife.

The Top 10 Reasons You Can Be Friends

1. Time has healed this wound.

2. You can hear him talk about new people he's dating and not throw up.

3. You had a great friendship before you dated.

4. You're absolutely, unequivocally not in love with him anymore.

5. You're ready to friend him again on Facebook, and won't have your heart torn out by seeing a picture of him at a party without you.

6. You look at your ex as a buddy you'd like hang out with and not as someone you want to have babies with.

7. The thought of having sex with him doesn't appeal to you whatsoever.

(continues)

(continued)

8. Even after several shots of tequila, you still wouldn't sleep with him.

9. Seeing him reminds you of why he did you a favor and why he wasn't right for you.

10. You're in a new, loving relationship and have let go of your old one.

How to Be Friends with Your Ex

Here are some tips to help you have a healthy friendship with your ex. They'll only work if you're *both* open and willing to make it work. The old relationship is gone and you are starting over with a new one. It's okay to go slow. This is new for you and him—it's like you're both learning to walk again. And friendships take time to develop. As long as it feels good and right, keep going. If it doesn't, stop and see why not. Maybe you're still hanging on to who you were with him, or haven't fully gotten over your feelings for him, or you're suddenly stalking him on Facebook again. If you see yourself slipping, take a giant step back. Go to the top of this chapter and start again. If you are ready, keep these tips in mind:

1. Be friends with yourself first. Be your best friend, ally, and supporter. Work on your own goals and develop your own interests. Hang out with your friends. Be happy with you and where you're at right now, because it's exactly where you're supposed to be.

2. See him for who he really is. See him as a person, not as the love of your life who tore your heart to pieces. See all of his imperfections, like his crooked nose, or how he slurps his soup, or that he's as cranky as his cockatoo (which is why they deserve each other). If you view him as the flawed guy you no longer want to date, it'll be easier to be friends with him. Also, you won't compare him to the next guy you go out with.

3. Show concern, but don't get involved. You can be a care bear without getting sucked into his drama or his life. Don't get involved in his job problems, his money issues, or his problems with his cantankerous parrot, because you don't have that kind of relationship anymore.

This was always tough one for me. After one particular breakup, this guy would pour his heart out to me over the phone about everything that was bothering him. We had a long history together, and so he'd call because he knew I understood him better than anyone. My heart would immediately go out to him. I'd listen and try to offer solutions. I'd wake up in the middle of the night, thinking about how I could help him. Finally, I had to learn to detach in order to have a conversation without getting emotionally caught up in his problems.

4. Don't talk about your past relationship. Past. Over. Gone. You don't need to rehash your breakup or relive the good times when you dated. Don't reminisce about the time you went to San Francisco and spent a romantic, rainy afternoon drinking Irish coffees and talking for hours. These kinds of conversations will keep you in the past. It may also make your ex feel uncomfortable since he just wants to be friends.

Instead, focus on common interests that made you compatible in the first place: your favorite football team, love of movies, skiing, music, or whatever. These topics are acceptable and won't get you into trouble.

5. No flirting. No crushing on him over drinks, sexting him, or drunk-dialing him in the middle of the night. Whether you're on your first glass of wine or your third, no amount of flirting, hand-holding, or affection of any kind with your ex is a good thing, no matter how good he looks in that Armani shirt.

I wasn't authentic in the relationship, but I am in the friendship. I get more as his friend than I ever did when I was dating him.

We have a great connection, but in love, it's just not a match.

—"Fran"

---

6. See your ex as a guy who dates. You have to be okay if he's dating a Barbie who's a size zero, or he's in a relationship with someone who looks like you. Make sure you can handle it. I know this is tough, but you need to be prepared when it happens. You have to be able to hear him talk about a new girl without wanting to throw a shoe at him.

7. See yourself as a girl who dates. As you cultivate this new friendship with your ex, you need to get out and date as well. Nothing can help you move on faster than hooking up with a new hottie. As long he's not Mr. Rebound or Mr. Get-Back-At-My-Ex-And-Make-Him-Jealous, you're good to go.

It may be tough at first to make the friend transition, but if you do it right, you'll have a good friend *and* a great life. Remember, he did you a favor by breaking up with you. The relationship wasn't working, but maybe the friendship will. I've developed friendships with many of my exes and they've been great.

How long will this new friendship with him last? Time will tell. I'm still friends with some of my exes, but others I only stayed friends with for a short time and then we drifted apart. Let your friendship take its natural course.

Just ask yourself one important question: is he worth keeping in your life? If he is, then go for it. If not, let him go.

> **He did you a favor because...you lost a bad boyfriend and may have found a much better friend.**

The Do-Yourself-a-Favor Workbook: Healthy Recipe for Being Friends with Your Ex

Combine all these ingredients:

1. You're not in love with him anymore.

2. You still like each other a lot.

3. You are strong and healthy in your own life.

Mix together.

Place in a warm oven (not hot).

Let bake for a while (time may vary) until fully cooked and safe to consume.

Place your new friendship on the table and enjoy.

Chapter 12

He Did You a Favor because He Gave You a Parting Gift.

Get ready to get rolling in gratitude, girlfriend. This is about receiving the gifts this past relationship gave you. Even if you haven't fully gotten over your breakup, being grateful can lift your mood, turn your thoughts around, and have you stepping on to the sunny side of the street.

You may be thinking, "How can I be grateful?" Remember, by breaking up with you he saved you a bunch of time. Time you might've wasted trying to patch up a bad relationship, feeling crappy about yourself, or wondering why you're not good enough. Your ex pulled the plug so you can now put your time towards being fabulous and finding a new man who thinks you're hot stuff on a shiny silver platter. Life is about being joyful. There's no joy in a relationship that isn't working, no matter how much you dress it up in pink bows and sparkles. Instead, how about unwrapping your new sparkly life?

After months of crying and "coming to terms" I became more alive, more present, and more focused. It was just my daughter and myself at home now, drawing at our coffee table, talking, reading, and making dinner together. It felt strangely invigorating. I was so unbelievably present with her. I realized I was happy, really happy. I was happy because I could start over again, and do it any way I wanted to but this time as this older and much wiser person. I could create a new and more fulfilling story for us.

Now, for the first time in years, I feel like I am awake and back on the right path. Everything seems brighter, like some foggy lens has been lifted from my eyes and I am now seeing clearly, and everything is in color again. Did my husband do me a huge favor by having an affair and showing me who he really is? My day to day is not as predictable as it had been with him, but I like it and it gives me a new sense of confidence that I have not felt in a long time. I can handle things on my own. I can raise a confident, smart daughter by myself with a lot of success. I can teach her that in life everyone goes through times of crisis, no one is immune, and how we behave and come out of that crisis is the most important. I can teach her not to struggle against things that don't go your way but instead be open to life, and it's unpredictability.

My daughter and I are in a new city now. We are starting over. I am in a relationship with an amazing man who knows who he is and allows me to be who I am. And I know my daughter and I are exactly where we are supposed to be.

—"Tess"

> **Breakup tip:** No matter how traumatic your breakup was, it's helping you to create a better life for yourself.

By seeing the gifts in your breakup, you are acknowledging the relationship for what it was and what you got out of it, plus you're empowering yourself to move on to bigger and better things!

> He gave you a huge gift wrapped in a big, red bow: the gift of *you*.

Go Ahead, Be Selfish

They say it's better to give than to receive, but it has to go both ways. So many of us give at the expense of ourselves. Consequently, we become tired and frustrated, needing love and assurance and wondering why we're not getting it. This self-sacrifice can turn into serious self-denial—giving up your precious, awesome self for another who you consider to be more important. Chances are, you gave a lot in this relationship and probably gave even more when it was falling apart to try to keep it together, all at the expense of you. In relationships, giving was my way of expressing love, but I was missing one key ingredient: *I didn't love myself as much as I loved him.*

Remember, your ex did you a favor by letting you go. No matter how perfect he seemed, if he didn't give you what you needed, it's time to move on to someone who will. Being selfish saves you time and heartache. It's about being powerful and taking control, as opposed to feeling weak and cheated. It's about taking care of you first.

> Selfish is the new black.

Being selfish doesn't mean being a self-centered narcissist. It means being true to *you*. Selfishness says you deserve more. It also says you're ready to receive much more from a man. Additionally, it means acknowledging the unique, amazing person that you are, so you can accept all the great gifts life has to offer you.

Finding the Gifts He Gave You

So how do you find the gifts specific to your traumatic breakup? Take a look back at all the things you could possibly be thankful for in this relationship, as well as what it's taught you about who you are and what you truly want.

Finding Gifts in the Jerky Things He Did

Let's first look at some gifts he could've given you that are not so easy to spot. They're ones you couldn't see until you broke up, because you were so blindly "in it" that you couldn't see the forest for the trees. Remember, if everything was hearts and flowers we'd never learn anything. So the jerky, stupid things he did in the relationship can teach you a lot.

> He gave you a gift—the gift of knowing. Knowing who you are and what you want.

Here are some examples of where his bad behavior, and maybe your less-than-stellar responses, can be something to be grateful for now:

- ✳ Did you learn what you want and don't want by him being an insensitive bonehead or an incessant critic?

- ✳ Did you learn that being needy or drowning in lack of self-worth has kept you dating a series of Mr. Cheater Bears? Are you ready to rock your self-worth now?

- ✳ Did you learn that you don't need to cater to a man's every need in order to be loved in return?

- ✳ Did you learn that dating a serial womanizer could kill your self-respect?

- ✳ Did you learn that his freeloading was emptying you and your wallet?

Now make your own list and be grateful you are out of this relationship. By breaking up with you, he gave you the opportunity to be happy (because chances are you haven't been for a while).

My friend set me up with this guy and we totally hit it off. After the third date, he said, "I keep my personal and business life very separate, so I'd appreciate it if you didn't tell anyone, especially your friends, anything about me personally." I didn't think much of it, so I said, "Okay. Sure." On our sixth date we were messing around and the following conversation took place:

Me: *"Before this goes anywhere, I want you to know I don't sleep around. I'm a germophobe. If I sleep with someone, we'll both have to get tested."*

Him: *"I feel exactly the same. I don't want you to be pressured. We can take things really slow. I have other girls for sex. What's important is that we found each other."*

Me: *"Wait. You have—other girls?"*

Him: *"Yeah."*

Me: *"More than two?"*

Him: *"Yeah, why?"*

Me: *"Wow. Thank you for telling me and for being so honest."*

Him: *"That's not going to change anything, right? I already told my therapist about you."*

Me: *"Oh, yeah, that totally changes everything!"*

He obviously wasn't ready for a relationship and clearly didn't want one. He wasn't willing to change, so I told him, "You've gotta go." Even though it hurt, I was so grateful for his honesty. It saved me a lot of wasted time and heartache.

Obviously, he did me a huge favor.

—"Tracy"

It's easier to let go of a relationship that's so clearly wrong for us, but what if it wasn't such a crappy relationship? What if everything had been going great before he dropped the breakup bomb? When my breakup happened, we had just returned from a great trip in Hawaii. Everything seemed to be fine, which is why I was blind-sided and why it was so hard for me to let go. But looking back, I could see there was more going wrong with us than going right. If you look close enough, you'll see it, too.

Now I know that, even if a relationship doesn't work out, I'm here to receive any gifts it has to offer. For that I am always grateful.

My gratitude is about sex and trust.

After I'd been abused, I was terrified of intimacy. The man I dated afterward, who I thought was the love of my life, also brought me back from the dead sexually and emotionally, because when we were together, he was patient, passionate, and completely there for me.

I was devastated when we broke up, but I'm so grateful he had the guts to do it, because we ultimately weren't right for each other long term. So, he did me two favors—he fell in love with me, and he left.

—"Jane"

Finding Gifts in the Good Things He Did

This isn't about reliving the good times so that you start obsessing again and grab a bottle of pinot grigio and handfuls of gummy bears. This is about being thankful so you can leave the past where it belongs—behind you—and so you can move forward.

The truth is, if this relationship had an impact on your life, then he gave you something. It could be something tangible. For example, I got my beautiful daughter. Or it could be something else. Think about what this relationship has taught you personally. Was there something he got you to try for the first time? Did you learn something new about yourself? Did he open you up in ways you never had been before? This is not to have you spiral into, "He's the most amazing guy in the world and why do I not have him in my life anymore"—remember, this is just to show you that this person was in your life for a reason. If you two were meant to be together you'd be picking out china.

> *I learned a lot from my ex. He introduced me to fine single malt scotches and great food. We shopped the countryside for heirloom peppers and artisanal honey. He taught me about mid-century modern furniture and Fiesta dinnerware. He opened up worlds to me I didn't know existed.*
>
> —"Natalia"

Here are some other gifts women accepted and received after their breakups:

* ✳ "I got the gift of discovering how powerful I am."
* ✳ "I got the chance to blossom into a new career."

* "My ex was such a gym jock, I'm now in the habit of exercising three times a week and I love it."

* "I got the gift of my two kids."

* "My ex gave me the gift of letting go so I could find the real love of my life. We've been married for five years and I couldn't be happier."

Say "Thank You"

You don't have to say it to his face, this is for *you*, not him. Be thankful this relationship ended, because you probably wouldn't have put the brakes on by yourself.

I would have never stepped fully into my writing career if my husband hadn't left. I wouldn't have developed the self-confidence I have now. The breakup helped me to break free from unhealthy patterns, so I could step into my passion and purpose in life. For that, I can thank him. I can also thank him for being a generous friend and a great father to our daughter.

> *Although there were some real painful moments in my relationship with my ex, I wouldn't change what happened because of all the gifts I discovered within me. I found my true, authentic, self and that is incredibly powerful—no one can take that away from me. It made me a stronger, better, more generous, loving person and for that, I am truly grateful.*
>
> —"Sally"

So be grateful because now you get to experience real love—the love of yourself and the awesome opportunity to love a more fabulous man!

Get Your Gratitude On

Say this three times out loud:

> *"Thank you for bringing this person into my life and for the lessons I've learned from the relationship. I am grateful for the experience and am ready to let go fully and freely. I am keeping my heart open for a more loving, satisfying relationship with someone who loves me for the incredible woman that I am."*

Additionally, once you've discovered and accepted the gifts this breakup has given you, don't slip backward because you feel unworthy. You deserve to be happy. You deserve a loving relationship. You deserve to have all your dreams come true. It can happen, if you believe you're worth it.

Start a Gratitude Journal

Start by getting a notebook in your favorite color. Every day, write five things you're grateful for. It could be your great apartment, your sweet dog, or your best friend. And if you're on a roll don't stop at five, keep going!

A little something about gratitude: keep expressing it and you'll get more of it.

Give Yourself a Gift

When I was a kid, I never had a problem asking for the things I wanted, whether it was a chocolate chip cookie or a new bike. The funny thing is, as we get older, it gets harder to ask for what we want and even harder to believe we'll get it. Don't block your desires. If you do, it's like wanting a new dress, then seeing exactly what you're looking for in a store window, but making all kinds of excuses about why you shouldn't try it on. Ask yourself, which makes you feel happier?

> **Favorable tip:** Believe you deserve all the gifts life has to offer.

Make a "wish list" of what you want in life. After you make your list, here's the important part: let go. It's all about allowing this or something even better to come into your life.

So toss a coin into the wishing well, wish on a star, or stick your wishes under your pillow. Most importantly, make them from your heart and feel they're already coming true.

Your Anytime Holiday Wish List

I wish for...

* An awesome career doing what I love.

* Time to travel more.

* A new man who loves and adores me.

Now make your own list! Believe like a kid again.

I've received everything on my wish list so far. I have incredible new friends who are caring and supportive. I'm doing what I love. I live in a beautiful home with my wonderful daughter. And I have a loving relationship with an amazing man who makes me a better woman. And I remind myself every day to say, "Thank you" for all the gifts in my life.

It's Your Birthday—The Birth of Your New Life!

Every ending is a brand-new beginning. So why not celebrate?

A girlfriend of mine threw herself a stellar divorce party at this swanky restaurant in Beverly Hills and invited a bunch of her friends. She got all dressed up and looked gorgeous. It was such a positive way to finalize her divorce and to celebrate her new life. She even had cake and champagne. It was the best party! We lit birthday candles and she made a wish and blew them out. That night she met a guy. He was so impressed with her that he asked her out.

Be grateful you are out of a relationship that no longer serves you, and serve yourself up some chocolate cake instead!

He did you a big favor. Being single simply rocks because you are fully free to design your life. So get some party favors, gather a few friends, and make some noise. Celebrate *you*!

> **He did you a favor because...he gave you the gift of freedom, renewed self-worth, and the opportunity to attract a better guy.**

The Do-Yourself-a-Favor Workbook: "I Am Awesome" Gratitude Cake

Ingredients:

1 box cake mix (your favorite flavor)

1 can pre-made frosting

You can do this from scratch using your grandmother's recipe, if that's what you're into, but for me, that's too much work.

Directions:

As you mix together the ingredients, think about all the great things in your life.

Pour the batter into a pan and bake. Use that time to take a "you" break—relax with a glass of wine, read a magazine, or catch up on your favorite TV show.

When it's ready, take it out. Let it cool (and be happy you chilled on this guy).

Frost (and think about how finding a new great guy will be the icing on your already fabulous cake).

Place five candles on top; one for each thing you're grateful for (say each one out loud).

Invite friends over. Light the candles and celebrate your delicious, sweet life!

Chapter 13

He Did You a Favor because Now You Get to Celebrate the Most Important Person in the World...You.

*Y*our wallowing days are over and your winning days are here. It's time for you to own the magnificent woman you are. Making it through this breakup and learning something about yourself shows that you've got what it takes to live a happy life filled with all you desire. So here you are; keep those radiant eyes looking forward because it's time to rock your life.

Own Your Fabulousness

Whether you see it or not, you're already fabulous—there's only one of you in the whole, entire world. That's pretty amazing. So embrace what's special about you. This is all about finding ways to feel confident and to show off what you've got. Then, if you bump into your ex at a bar (it's a small world—it happens) he'll be blown away by you, Miss Awesome. He may even want you back, which could be such sweet revenge, but you won't care because you're way past this guy now. Moving on was the best thing you could've done for yourself.

Your Beautiful Face

Look in the mirror. What do you see? Is it a beautiful, radiant woman, or someone who's overstressed, overtired, or just older ("When did *that* happen?")? Or you see that huge pimple on your chin, all those freckles, or maybe it's just that the mirror is dirty and needs cleaning.

When you look at yourself in the mirror, let go of what bothers you, as well as anything you don't like. Seriously, your flaws are not your problem or concern. Besides, what you focus on, you create. So freaking out about the slightest wrinkle on your forehead will only make you frown and make it worse.

The truth is that every face is unique, which is what makes each of us beautiful. So look in the mirror again. This time, pick one or two things you love and focus on them for several seconds. By shifting your attention to your favorite feature(s), those flaws and imperfections you perceive will fade into the background. I've done it and it works. When I focus on my green eyes, suddenly I'm not obsessing about my nose. If you slip, and suddenly can't stop looking at that mole on your forehead, stop and refocus. Do this face exercise every day.

Additionally, keep in mind that our imperfections are what make us special. No one wants someone who's perfect. Perfect is boring. Imperfection is beautiful.

> **Beauty tip:** Look at yourself in the mirror every morning and say, "Hi, gorgeous"...and mean it.

Your Great Body

Beauty comes in all shapes and sizes, so stop picking your body apart. Obsessing about your weight, the size of your butt, or your big feet doesn't do you any good and takes up precious time. Besides, you could miss out on dating that great new guy because you're (way too) busy worrying about your thighs.

So get over your body hang-ups and hold on to what you like best instead. Wear those jeans that hug your great curves, or that little black dress that flatters your figure and everyone always compliments you on, or that blue jacket that brings out your blue eyes. Your clothes are an expression of who you are and your body should feel confident in them.

And by the way, Spanx is your best friend—let it do its job and don't feel guilty about it. This is about delegating, so you don't have to hold in your stomach *and* smile.

So respect your body and take good care of it. It's the only one you have. Always remember it's your ally, not your enemy.

Your Sexy Attitude

Now let's move on to the one thing that will make all the difference—it's what's on the inside that really counts.

Do you remember a time when you were having a great day and someone said how great you looked? Nothing changed except how you felt. Feelings are everything. A woman who feels beautiful, looks beautiful. A woman who feels confident, looks confident. A woman who feels sexy... well, you get it now.

Favorable tip: Confidence is your best accessory.

I knew this guy who fell for two women at once. He seriously agonized over which one to choose. He would break up with one, then get back together with her, and break up with the other. It went on for six months. They both should've dumped him, but neither knew what was going on (although they probably suspected). One woman was blond, model-gorgeous, and shared all his interests. The other woman was a cute brunette who shared only some of his interests. Well, guess what? He went with the brunette. Why? Because she was fun, confident, and made it clear that she didn't care whether he stayed or left. The blond was insecure and held on to him far too tight. The happy ending is that he and the brunette have been happily married for 10 years.

So get ready to rock your sassy attitude. How do you get there? Here are some terrific tips:

Acknowledge where you're great. It's so easy for us to acknowledge others, but we don't often do it for ourselves. So make a self-acknowledgment list to celebrate you and all that you do. It doesn't have to be just for those milestone accomplishments, but also for those daily tasks you've crossed off your "to do" list. For example:

✳ I acknowledge myself for writing 5 pages.

* I acknowledge myself for cleaning out my closet and getting better organized.

* I acknowledge myself for eating healthy.

* I acknowledge myself for working out on the elliptical for 30 minutes.

* I acknowledge myself for getting a massage and taking better care of *me*.

Write three to five acknowledgements at the end of each day and you'll gain motivation and confidence to accomplish your big goals.

Remember something that made you happy. Think about an amazing trip you took, or how much you love to water ski, or a moment when you accomplished something that made you feel terrific. Sit with that thought for a few minutes and feel like it's happening again right now. It'll give your happiness level an instant boost.

Compare yourself to no one. No one can do a better job of being you than you. So, if you feel the urge to compare yourself to someone else, stop and redirect your focus within. Concentrate on all your good qualities. Compare where you were last year to where you are today. Or think about something you accomplished, or where you've made changes for the better. How are you becoming a new and improved you?

See the beauty in others. This is important because women can be so judgmental of each other. So, instead of seeing a woman rockin' her size two Gucci dress and criticizing, thinking that her dress is too snug or feeling jealous that her belly is flatter than yours, see the beauty in her and smile. If you love her hair, her handbag, or her funky nail polish, you could even go over and tell her. By feeling great for her, you become more beautiful yourself.

One time, I saw this woman wearing this beautiful, long skirt as I was coming out of the grocery store. She stared back at me, but we didn't say anything. Suddenly, I felt self-conscious. I thought, "Does she think I'm weird for staring? Is she angry at me for some reason? Do I have something on my face?" Finally, she said, "I love your dress!" I responded, "I love your skirt!" We talked for a few minutes about how women are so reluctant to give compliments. She was really sweet and not the aloof "mean girl" I imagined her to be. Afterward, I felt great for the rest of the day.

Receive compliments. Receiving a compliment can be as difficult as trying to run a marathon in high heels. We'll dodge, deflect, and downplay it until there's nothing left. For example, if someone says, "I love your hair," you may respond:

* "It's too frizzy."

* "Actually, I need a haircut."

* "My roots are showing."

What we say affects how we think and how we act. I still catch myself sometimes either making excuses or quickly lobbing it back by saying, "I love your hair, too." This isn't a tennis match. A compliment is a gift given to you. Do you really want to toss it back? And if you do, how do you think that makes the other person feel? They may not only feel bad for saying it, they may think twice before giving you another one.

How to Receive a Compliment

* Listen.

* If you feel the urge to deflect it, stop yourself.

* Receive the compliment.

* Smile and say, "Thank you."

Simple, right? So the next time someone gives you a compliment, take it and see how great it feels.

Give your confidence a quick facelift. Whether you inherently have the confidence gene or not, everyone can learn self-confidence. Even if you're not feeling it now, try this simple trick: fake it until you make it. Even faking confidence will put you in the right frame of mind. Eventually, you'll get there for real.

Also, simply sitting up straight can help you feel more confident.

Feel okay in any situation. So you had an icky day. Your boss was unscrupulously demanding, your ex-boyfriend nabbed an assignment you wanted (ouch), or you accidently broke the coffee machine and now your coworkers are coming at you with stir sticks like a lynch mob. Or maybe you found out that the guy you've been flirting with just asked one of your friends out. Disappointing days suck, but just remember if the job you interviewed for or the assignment you worked to get is meant to be yours, it will be. If not, something better will come along. The same goes for a guy you've been flirting with. If he's not asking you out, someone better will show up.

Even if you made a bad blunder that day, give yourself a break. Know you did the best you could at the time. No head pounding or self-flagellation is needed here. Tomorrow is another day.

The best part of any day is you get to go home and be with the best person in the world—*you.*

Favorable tip: In any situation you can be defeated or determined, forceful or forgiving, powerless or empowered. It's your choice to make.

Seize every opportunity. Even if you're not sure, give every new opportunity a chance before you reject it. Don't waste time sitting at home agonizing about the pros and cons of joining an adult soccer team, or going on an interview or a blind date. Otherwise, you may wake up the next day with a load of regret, instead of waking up with a big smile on your face because you took a chance.

Believe in the Life You Want and Start Living It Now

Remember, at any moment you are free to choose the life you want to live. Every day is a new day to be fabulous. So why not start right now? Here are some tips to get you going.

Envision What You Want

Our brains think in pictures, which is why vision boards can be so powerful. Think hieroglyphics—cavemen were on to something! It's a great way to imagine the life you want. So grab your scissors, a glue stick, and a stack of your favorite magazines (fashion, travel, fitness, whatever you're into). Cut out pictures of people, places, and things that inspire you: a beach bungalow in Malibu, an adoring guy embracing a smiling girl, a glass of red wine in a vineyard in Italy. Dream bold. Dream big. Dream bigger. Take these visions of inspiration and glue them on a poster board. You could even have a board party night with your girlfriends. When you're done, put your board somewhere where you can look at it every day.

Live Passionately

Be passionate in everything you do, whether it's writing your novel, picking out a piece of artwork, or enjoying an incredible meal you cooked. To tap into your passion, answer these questions:

1. **What do you love to do?** Play guitar? Ice-skate? Cook gourmet French meals? Dance like they do in music videos? Make giant sculptures out of papier-mâché?

It doesn't matter right now whether you're doing what you love professionally or not; what matters is that your passion fuels your purpose in life. So whether you're a rock star playing in a stadium, or a rock star in a karaoke bar, or a rock star in your own living room, it's the act of doing it that matters. I love to dance. Sometimes, I just put on music and dance around my living room for 15 minutes. It gets my heart pumpin', makes me happy, and I feel great afterward. Sometimes it's just what I need to kick start my day or to get me out of my three-o'clock rut.

2. What would be your perfect day? Is it a hike in the morning followed by dinner with friends? Or a spa day, followed by yoga class? Or is it lounging at the beach with a good book, then hooking up later with your BFF for a movie? Whatever it is, do it. Pick a day to indulge yourself—and don't feel guilty about it.

3. What's a simple moment you can relish right now? Maybe it's enjoying strawberry frozen yogurt with crushed Oreo cookies, or making yourself a peanut butter and banana greenie shake (my favorite), or playing Frisbee with your dog. It's your moment, so you choose. This simple, 10-minute boost can be just what you need to brighten your day.

You may be thinking, "I'm too busy, I don't have time for any of this." Yes, you do. Make time.

A girlfriend of mine in Los Angeles spent hours dating online with no success. This only made her more disillusioned and depressed. Her passion was singing, so one day, she decided to throw a Baby Grand Party. She hired a piano player, and invited people to come over and sing their favorite songs. The night went incredibly well. Not only that, she was happy, confident, and glowing all night. One of her friends brought a guy to the party. The next day he emailed this friend saying how amazing he thought she was. Also, the night was such a huge success she decided to host several more. This guy came to every one. He was so taken by her; he just had to ask her out.

The only difference in her was that she focused on her passion and was joyful in sharing it with others. She wasn't even thinking about meeting a man. Consequently, the man showed up.

> **Favorable tip:** Stop looking for love and start doing *what* you love...then love will find you.

Set Your Intentions

Creating your dreams begins with setting your intentions. It's important to be clear about what you desire. For example, you could start your day with:

* I intend to eat a healthy breakfast.

* I intend to have a creative, productive day.

* I intend to have a fun, enjoyable night out.

* I intend to have restful, relaxing sleep tonight.

The more you set your intent before action, the better focus and clarity you will have, and the better results you will see.

> *I'm good at stating my intentions, but sometimes they get muddled.*
>
> *Recently, I wrote down all of my intentions and was trying to figure out where to put them. I had all these flowers I needed to plant, and I thought, "What could be better than planting my intentions?" So I put them under my flowers. Now I water them and just let them grow.*
>
> —*"Carrie"*

On the flip side, remember expectation leads to disappointment. Many times, we set the bar way the heck too high, expecting others to reach it. This'll set you (and your next relationship) up for failure. Think about it this way: how many times have you expected someone to do something and he or she didn't do it? How did that make you feel? Sad? Hurt? Angry? How many times have you expected a job to turn out a certain way, but instead it turned into something else?

Set your intentions, but be open, flexible, and ready for the unexpected to happen, as well.

Shake Up Your Routine

What have you always wanted to do but have never done? Learn photography or a foreign language? Take a Piloxing or pole-dancing class? Go Parasailing or scuba diving? One of my favorite sayings is, "Feel the fear and do it anyway." Don't think about it, just do it.

Spruce Up Your Place

By changing up your woman cave, you'll be changing up your life, as well. This is important especially if you lived with Mr. Ex-Heartbreaker and he used the living room as his office (and you still have pushpin holes in the walls), or he left his hubcap coffee table and you haven't moved it yet (or you can't move the darn thing because it weighs a ton), or you're staring at the mismatched shelves he built for his German beer stein collection.

It's time to fully reclaim your space. Here are a few things you can do:

1. Do some spring cleaning, even if it's the dead of winter. Get rid of any clutter that's piling up in corners or closets. Clearing out the old to make room for the new can also give your thoughts and feelings a fresh start.

2. Move stuff around. Move around furniture, pictures, lamps, books, or sculptures—whatever. Rearranging your stuff will give you a new perspective.

3. Freshen up your space. You don't have to spend a ton of cash, just paint a wall, or get some bright pillows, a new rug, or some fun lamps. You could buy some fresh flowers, change out your old pictures for new ones, or maybe host a "picture party" with friends (yes, I'm suggesting another party, Miss Get Out And Be Social). You could also take new pictures and display those. A couple of years after my breakup, I threw a holiday party, took tons of pictures with a group of great friends, had a bunch of 8×10s framed, and hung them in my hallway.

Even now when I look at them, I feel happy, loved, and supported.

It takes courage to live a fabulous life, and trust that you've got courage in spades, girl! Live freely and love passionately. Wake up every day with hope and happiness for your future.

> **He did you a *big* favor because...now you get to truly appreciate and celebrate *you*.**

The Do-Yourself-a-Favor Workbook: Your "New You" Party

* Have a champagne and dessert party and invite your closest friends.

* Let them write down their wishes for you on mini–gift cards and drop them in a crystal bowl (and you can do the same for them).

* Read, receive, and enjoy!

Chapter 14

He Did You a Favor because You Get to Shop for a Better Man.

Now that you're feeling good and you know what you want in a man, take your dating life off hold. You're done being a coach potato, so take off your breakup sweats and get dressed. Get out of your woman cave. Step out as the incredible woman you are and get the guy you desire.

Who's Your Dream Guy?

When I was a kid, I played the game *Mystery Date* with my girlfriends. We'd take turns opening up that mystery door to see whether we got the dream guy in the white tux, the hot surfer dude, or the scruffy dud. Every time I got the dud, my girlfriends would point and laugh, making me feel even worse.

Unlike *Mystery Date*, your ultimate fate is not lef* chance. In life, you have a choice. If you end ﹀ dud, you don't have to waste valuable tir door on that sucker and try again. Eventually, your dream guy will show up. So let's get clear on Mr. Dreamboat.

Your Dream Guy Wish List

Write down 100 things you'd like your guy to be. You may get stuck after a while, but keep going. I got stuck after 50, but by digging deeper and getting specific I came up with them all.

After you've written yours, stick the list in an envelope, seal it, and put it away. Yep, I said put it away. Why?

Because, again, here's the most important part: *Let go.* You've described what you want in a man very clearly. Great. But remember, this is a wish list, not a checklist. Be open for this or someone better to come along.

Women I know have done this exercise and were amazed by the guys who appeared in their lives afterward. Heck, it's worth a try, right? So get writing, girlfriend!

New Spots to Find Mr. Oh-So-Right

Okay, you are ready to dip your toes back in the dating pool. Here are some fun ways to get you going:

Do something different. If you've always hung out at bars or scanned Facebook for your next date, why not try something different? Get creative. Do something new. For example, if you're the outdoor type, take a rock climbing class. If you love golf, grab some friends and go play a few rounds. If you like vintage furniture, go to an antique auction. There's so much you can do and have fun at the same time—beach volleyball, book fairs, or take a trip somewhere you've always wanted to go. A friend of mine went on a trip to Cabo San Lucas to relax and "get away from it all." Her first day there she met a guy. They married a year later.

Come up with some great ideas of your own. And when you go, remember: this should be playtime, not you-working-hard-to-find-your-right-guy time. That'll come not only when you're in the right place, but when it's the right time as well.

Enlist your friends. It's the six-degrees school of thought. Right now you're probably six degrees or less away from the man you're meant to be with. I met my guy through one of my close friends. They'd known each other for over 10 years, and yet we'd never met. We were even at the same party two years earlier, but he was dating some-one else, and I was so busted up from my breakup I kept to myself and only socialized with the people I knew. Consequently, I didn't even see him.

Here are other ways to recruit your friends:

* Have a party and ask each friend to bring some-one new. By doing this, you could be helping your single friends make a match as well!

* If your friend is meeting co-workers for happy hour or a baseball game, ask if you can tag along.

* Be bold. Just ask friends if they know a great guy for you!

Be open and ready anytime, anywhere. Your next great date can come from anywhere: the laundromat, the mall, or the market (everyone's gotta eat, right?). So look good whenever you go out. Even if you're in sweats, make sure they're fab, like Juicy Couture, and that you feel great in them.

> *Whenever I go to this one Trader Joe's, I'm amazed by how many hot guys shop there. Seriously. It's crazy. One time I was having a party, so I was buying a lot of food and wine. As I was walking around with a cart full of party provisions, guys would say, "Can I come over to your house?" One guy even helped me with a wine selection. I ended up inviting him to my party and we dated for several months. Even though it ended, I still go to that Trader Joe's whenever I have a party. They still have great stuff, cute guys, and I always leave there feeling great.*
>
> —"Sherri"

So next time you go to the grocery store, why not check out the meat section? See a grilling-master guy lingering by the steaks? Ask him which one's a good cut, or if T-bone is better than Porterhouse. You never know.

Playing the Dating Game

It's time to get suited up and get in the game. Here are some winning game tips:

Girls just want to have fun. When you walk into a room with confidence and no agenda, that's when you get noticed. Think about it—how many times have you *not* been looking and the guy just showed up? On the other hand, if you're desperate to find The One and start asking a guy what his sign is, if he wants to have kids, or what his ex was like, then he'll make his exit, quick.

Again, think of all the ways you're awesome and let them shine. Be authentic and be proud of who you are. A woman who lives a full, passionate life and who clearly doesn't need a man, gets the guy, every time. Trust me. It'll also get you that much deserved promotion, dream job, or apartment...whatever!

Favorable tip: Self-confidence is a dude magnet.

Leave your insecurities at the door. Guys don't focus on a woman's flaws, so you shouldn't focus on yours. You should feel like all that and a bag of chips, and not like you've eaten too many chips. So, don't announce how you hate your thighs, your flabby arms, or moan that you had a Big Mac and a shake and feel incredibly bloated. If you don't say it, the guy you're talking to won't notice it. If he does, he's so not for you. Ditch that superficial lame-o, quick.

Play the mystery game. Don't spill all the details about yourself in one shot. Don't reveal that you know the names and birthdates of all the guys who've been on *The Bachelor,* or that you've Pinterested your dream wedding, or how you can whistle through your nose. It's too much information.

Also, if you haven't already done it, lock your Facebook page. Don't allow the cute guy you just met to be able to go home and read your personal profile, or see pictures of you with your ex (which you better have deleted by now), or an embarrassing photo of you in a bunny suit at Halloween. Yikes. Let him get to know you, face to face.

Be genuinely you. While you're holding off spilling every little thing about yourself, also don't try to be something you're not to impress him. First dates can be tricky. Your desire to be liked could lead you to be someone you're not. You may create this persona because you think it will impress him. But it won't. Because remember, if you're not being authentically who you are, it'll come back to bite you when you're true colors show through later.

Play the numbers game. Men like to work for what they get, because it's more rewarding and they'll value it more. So give a guy the chance to ask for your digits. If he's interested, he will. If he's Mr. Super Shy and not so sure you're into him, make your intentions clear. Unless he's completely clueless, he's not into you, or he's gay, he'll get it and act on it.

When A New Guy Comes into Your Life

Okay, so you're attracted to a guy and there's definitely a spark between you two, but now what? Is he The One? Only time will tell. Right now he's a guy you like and you're dating, so just go with it. This is a time when everything's new, you're both on your best behavior, and you find yourself smiling every time you think of him. This is much more fun than Mr. Heartbreaker, right?

Relax and have fun. This is most important. This new guy could be a short-term relationship, a long-term boyfriend, or your future husband. It doesn't matter. Your first date shouldn't be a marriage tryout, an ex-boyfriend comparison evaluation, or any kind of major relationship test. If you're too busy testing him and grading his exam, you're missing out on really getting to know this guy. Just have fun and then see if he's worth a second (or third) date. By now, you've let go of all your past relationship baggage. If you haven't, then dump those suitcases full of neglect and regret and jump into this new adventure, free and clear.

No virtual snooping. Yes, I know you're excited by this new potential and want to know everything about him, but save it for dinner conversations. No cyber-spying. It's important to get to know your guy face to face and not be swayed by a photo you saw that you misinterpreted, or a blurb you saw on his home page that you read out of context.

I almost broke up with a guy I was dating because, silly me, I thought it'd be fun to check his Facebook page and learn more about him. Big mistake. Instead of seeing pictures of him doing silly things with his buddies, I saw pictures of him at parties with pretty women, and read messages from them saying, "I miss you." That was death for me, since those three words are how I found out about my husband's affair. We'd only been dating a month and it was going well, but I was ready to kick him to the curb.

Then, I took a deep breath and thought, "You don't know what you don't know." I got off his Facebook and never looked back. Later, I discovered these women were just friends and he ended up being Mr. Monogamous. There was never a problem with trust. I had manufactured something about his personality that didn't exist at all.

Master the sex game. It's great to flirt and rock what you've got, but don't give yourself away too soon. I know this seems obvious, but sometimes we get caught up in the moment and forget. Take time (meaning go on a few honest-to-goodness dates) and then decide when and if he deserves the rest of you. If you give in too soon, he's won an early victory. Get to know him first. If he's an honest guy with an ounce of integrity, he'll wait if you ask him to. If he keeps pushing after the first date, he's doing you a favor by showing you who he really is. Cut him loose, because this one's definitely not a keeper.

I've woken up in strange beds with guys who were either super clingy cuddle bears, or who served me coffee and then showed me the door. Neither morning wake up was any fun and none of those dates ever became a lasting relationship.

On the other hand, if your chemistry is off the charts and you just want a random night of hot sex, then go for it. If you want more, hold off.

> **Sex tip:** Don't bare your naked bodies until you've shared your naked selves.

Be attentive and aware. If things come up and comparisons are made to your ex, just say to yourself, "Good to know." You can decide later whether this new guy's know-it-all attitude is a red flag, or something you can live with (remember, if it's one of your deal-breakers don't break that deal with yourself). Also, be aware of certain undesirable patterns you may be repeating such as catering to his needs, not speaking up, or allowing him to criticize you. If you're repeating a negative pattern with this guy, change it, or find out why this guy's bringing it out in you, and if he's really right for you. Don't lose what you've learned from your past relationship. Instead use it to have a better relationship this time.

Give him a chance. By now you're clear on what your boundaries are and what you require. These standards can be his, as well, or not. If they're not, at least give him a chance before you kick him out the door. Allow him to step up and give you what you want. If he's interested, he will. If not, you know what to do.

Also, remember that expecting him to do what you want when you haven't made it clear is also unrealistic. People show love and affection in different ways. You may show love by being affectionate in public, while he may show it by doing something nice for you like giving you a foot massage, running an errand for you, or washing your dog. Understand that he's showing how much he cares in his way; be open to receiving it.

Is He Dateable?

Here's a simple quiz to see if this new guy's worth spending *all* your date nights with. You may not get all the answers right away, but after you've seen him several times, you should be able to determine if this guy is dateable or not.

Your Dating Quiz

1. Does he want to know about you, or does he talk about himself all the time?

2. Does he listen and ask questions?

3. Does he encourage or drain you?

4. Is he comfortable in his own skin, or is he jumping out of his skin?

5. Does he seem to support your goals, or make you doubt them?

6. Is he kind? Is he nice to everyone? Or is he sweet to you but rude to the wait staff?

7. Is he reliable? Does he show up on time for your date, or is he an hour late?

8. Is he proactive? Does he make reservations, or does he just show up at a restaurant that has a waiting list a mile long? Do you then have to wait for 2½ hours for a table, now fighting a stomach ache from eating too many peanuts at the bar because you're so frickin' starving?

(continues)

(continued)

9. Does he leave a great tip or a sucky tip? Or does he just leave and expect you to take care of the bill?

10. Does he break one or more of your deal-breakers even before the first kiss?

Now make your own personal date quiz. Don't be a stick in the mud, just stick to the important things.

Is He Mr. Right or Mr. Right Now?

If he turns out to be Mr. Right, great; jackpot! But if he turns out to be Mr. Right Now and it ends, know that he did you a favor. Be thankful for the experience, think about what you learned, and consider how you'll do things differently next time. Because there will be a next time with someone better, if you choose. Know that you deserve to be with someone who truly values and appreciates you.

Always remember the most important person is *you*. You are fabulous all on your own. The guy you date is just the cherry on top.

A Final Note about Your Ex

There may come a time after you've fully moved on when your ex pops up unexpectedly. Maybe you get a call on your anniversary because he just wants to "touch base" and "catch up." I've had several ex-boyfriends pop up out of nowhere to let me know they'd been thinking about me.

Some would occasionally send me flirty messages. Others just wanted to say, "Merry Christmas," or "Happy New Year." Remember, men need self-assurance too and will contact an ex-girlfriend to give their ego a boost. That's all it is. None of my ex's messages ended up with us getting back together. So if your ex calls six months later, the same rules apply now that did when you split up. Don't develop relationship amnesia and forget all the things that broke you up in the first place. Remember, if he doesn't love you the way you deserve to be loved, he's not worth your time. On the other hand, if you consider him a friend and you're absolutely not in love with him anymore, then it's okay to text, "Happy New Year," because it *is* a Happy New Year... with a happier new you. You now know he did you a favor.

A Final Note about You

So there you go, Miss Fabulous. You've gone from the kitchen floor pity party to stepping out in your high heels and kicking some serious butt in the world. Now you know that, if a relationship ends, he did you a favor. Equipped with the knowledge you've gained, you'll be able to move forward with courage, clarity, and renewed confidence.

If you ever find yourself slipping, you can always refer to this book. Rely on it the way you rely on your BFF, using it for advice or a loving kick-in-the-butt whenever you need it. You could occasionally get stuck in old habits or bad patterns. It happens all the time. But instead of grabbing that emotional sledgehammer, let this book help you get back on track. It'll remind you that Mr. Complicated is not going to simplify his life to be with you, or Mr. Let's-Keep-Things-Casual is not going to suddenly decide to play house with you, or that Mr. Casanova who wants several lovers...well, shove that one out the dog door. It'll remind you to use your intuition and to pay attention to your thoughts and feelings. It'll remind you that every mistake is an opportunity to become even better. It'll remind you what an incredible woman you are and that the guy you date better be incredible, too.

You may not use every word in this book. That's okay. Some chapters will resonate with you more than others. Whenever I coach writers, I always tell them, "Use what notes you can, the rest let go of." Why? Because whatever they're working on is uniquely their experience. They've lived with their project and know it better than anyone. I say the same to you. You know yourself better than anyone, so use what works best for you.

If you take one thing away, I hope it's that, in *any* situation, however powerless you feel, you always have a choice. You can be the victim and curl up under a blanket with a box of bonbons, or you can be the victor and get busy healing so you can move forward in a powerful way into the greater life you're meant to live.

You deserve to love and be loved. It is your birthright. Don't ever forget that. Don't ever forget what a super woman you are.

I wrote this book because I want you to succeed. After my divorce, my life changed in ways I never imagined because I realized he did me a favor. And so I was able to move on, knowing my life would be better for it. And I was right.

I want you to be empowered by your experience, as well. I want you to see that every occurrence in your life, good or bad, is an opportunity for growth. They *all* did you a favor. You are who you are today because of everything you've learned so far. Because of that, you can always move forward with confidence and gratitude.

Now it's time to get out there and enjoy your beautiful life. Have tons of fun. Do something new and unexpected, and don't look back. Remember, your power is in the present. It's in what you choose to do right here, right now. Life is filled with possibilities and you are ready for them all! See the opportunities everywhere. They're there if you look.

So, get your Warrior Woman on. Get out there and be absolutely fabulous. I know you can.

> **He did you a *big* favor because...now you have the opportunity to date men who truly appreciate you for the incredible woman you are!**

The Do-Yourself-a-Favor Workbook: How to Shop for a Man

1. Before you go out, make sure you're feeling good. If you feel bloated, or had a sucky day at work, or just got a bad haircut, then it's best to wait another day to go man shopping.

2. When shopping for a man, try a new place you haven't tried before. Just be sure it fits your personality. What I mean by this is, don't get season tickets to football if you hate sports. Don't go to the opera if it bores you to tears. Don't go skiing if the cold makes you grumpy. You'll not only be miserable, you'll be giving the wrong impression and make a man think you're into something you're not.

3. Don't get hung up on hanger appeal—he may look good from afar, but you won't really know until you try him on and get a feel for him. Don't be fooled by superficial charms, like his dazzling smile or his incredible sense of style. Look at him in the right light so you can see him for who he is and not who you want him to be. Make sure his qualities underneath are just as good as the ones outside.

That goes for online dating, as well. He may look classy and sophisticated on the web, but once you meet him in person, he may be a cheap knock-off whose bloated ego is way overpriced. If you date him anyway, it'll be at the expense of yourself.

4. Try someone you've never tried before. Have you ever seen a dress on a hanger and thought it wouldn't look good on you, but then someone suggests you try it on and it looks fabulous? The same goes for man shopping—even if you don't think he's right initially, try him anyway (just meet for coffee). You could be surprised how well he fits and how great you are with him.

5. If he's not a fit, don't buy into him hoping he'll fit better later. And don't try force anything to make him fit. Think about it this way: you may like that leopard print dress, but do large spotted cats really look good on you? Or that skin tight, leather mini skirt? Or those skinny jeans that show too much of your butt when you sit down?

Put Mr. Doesn't Fit back on the rack and let someone else try him on. There are plenty of other single men out there. Just keep on shopping.

Remember, when shopping for a man, you are free to return or exchange him any time you wish with no restocking charges. Only keep the guy who makes you look and feel like a million bucks. Happy man shopping!

The Do-Yourself-a-Favor Workbook: How To Find the Favors Everywhere In Your Life

You don't lift balloons at the gym to get stronger; you lift heavy weights. So, you never gain personal strength without great challenges. With this in mind, try this exercise:

1. Recall a painful, disappointing, or just plain sucky moment you've had in your life.

2. Think about what strength, insight, or quality you may have gained from that experience.

You may jump to a negative thought at first, but that's okay. Since now you know to look for the favor, spend some time discovering what you obtained from that experience.

Even now, I always remind myself there's a gift inside of all the painful experiences in my life (business or personal). Even if it's not immediately visible, I'll keep searching until I find it. And you know what? I always do.

Bonus: 10 Awesome Reasons "He Did You a Favor"

Okay, just to remind you one last time that he did you a favor, here are some favors received from my interviews with women. To find out more and stay updated on the latest news, go to *www.hedidyouafavor.com*. Log on any time you need a reminder that you are truly amazing.

"He Did Me a Favor Because..."

1. "That intense relationship made me stronger and more self-loving."

2. "Because of my breakup, I have much more clarity on my life."

3. "I learned to stand up for myself."

4. "I learned self-empowerment."

5. "I learned to stop repeating old patterns and start creating new ones."

6. "He forced me to get out of that town and find a new life. And I'm so glad I did."

7. "I got back the confident, creative woman I was before I got married."

8. "I grew into myself and found out what was missing all along."

9. "I never would have met the man I'm with now if I didn't learn from my past experience."

10. "He showed me the girl I didn't want to be. And now I'm the best woman I can be."

Much love to you,
Debra

Acknowledgements

To my fabulous life coach and dear friend, Andrea Quinn: you held my sword for me when I was too weak to and kept the light on my path until I was able to navigate it on my own. To Elizabeth DeVries for your love and guidance in helping to heal my broken heart. To Rosa Aguiar for all your help and for being there during my darkest times. To Gigi Ullah for our early morning conversations which sparked the title of this book. To my friends and family for all your love and support during this incredible, emotional journey. To the very talented "Scriptwrights" group, who supported me while I took a break from screenplays to pen this book. To my fabulous editors Karen Frank and Elizabeth Campbell—you gals simply rock. To Crystal Patriarche, Heidi Hurst, and everyone at BookSparks. To Julie Metz for her boundless creativity and helpful advice. To Christopher Daniels for his incredible talents. To the brilliant Maureen Forys at Happenstance Type-O-Rama. To Marc Friedland, for being a creative genius and for "getting it" from the start. To David Guillod and Amy Baer who believed in this project in its early stages and encouraged me to keep going with their unbridled enthusiasm. To Jen Sincero, my book coach: your powerful guidance kept me moving toward the finish line.

To all the women who went through their own heartbreaks and who were courageous enough to share their stories—you all are truly amazing and inspiring.

To my love, Scott: you are my knight and so much more. I appreciate all that you've done to help with the book *and* help me stay sane in the process! To my beautiful daughter Nicole, who inspires me every day of my life.

And finally, to my ex-husband, who did me a favor. Thank you.

I love you all.

Made in the USA
Las Vegas, NV
26 November 2020